Lit

an anthology of dynamic new monologues for
actors from underrepresented ethnicities

Published May 2022 by Team Angelica Publishing,
an imprint of Angelica Entertainments Ltd

Team Angelica Publishing
51 Coningham Road
London W12 8BS

TEAM
ANGELICA

www.teamangelica.com
A CIP catalogue record for this book is available from
the British Library

ISBN 978-1-9163561-6-0

LOTTERY FUNDED

Supported using public funding by

**ARTS COUNCIL
ENGLAND**

Disclaimer/Reclaimer

It's weird, after years of teaching so many actors to write business letters that avoid over-using the words 'I', 'Me' and 'My', if at all, to now be writing these forewords infested with I, I, I. But you know what? Even though this trilogy of books have been lovingly assembled as heartfelt offerings to the reader, and as showcases for the 200 brilliant writers who have poured themselves into every word, it's become so clear to me, me, me, that that this project, this labour of love, in which every word is written by someone else - is deeply personal.

I used to say, 'I don't want to be a black writer. Or a gay writer. Or a working class writer. I just want to be a writer.' Now I look back and think why not? Why did I think that being flavourless was radical? Why was I denying my herbs and spices? Why did I think my various perspectives and nuances were a distraction or deficit? Lots of writers think that way. Actors too. But who we are is not a limitation. It's a launch pad. It's an advantage. And lots of emerging creatives seem to be realising that fact more and more. Actors call out on social media for audition/showcase speeches that they can relate to. They write me emails asking for recommendations for working class monologues, LGBTQIA+ monologues, black, brown, Asian monologues. And more. I give them what I've written. But it's not enough. Try as I might, I haven't written enough or read enough to cover all the bases, to offer up all the nuances. What's needed is more writers.

And so we put out a call on social media for emerging writers (many of whom are actors themselves) who'd like to be mentored on how to write a great audition speech for queer actors, working class actors and/or underrepresented ethnicities... And so, six months and countless phone/WhatsApp feedback sessions later, we have these three books: *Fierce*, *Common* and *Lit*. Every speech is 3 minutes or less. Each one has its own attitude and vibe. Posh black voices, rural gay voices, educated council estate voices, stereotypes and anti-stereotypes and everything in between. Voices as various and complex as yours. This collection of speeches is for you. They're meant to be said, not read. Read 'em out loud. Whisper them. Shout them. Stretch them. Sing them. Bring them to life. Smash the audition. Stop the show. Be as gay or ethnic as you feel like being. Code switch. Nuance. Clarify. Enlighten. Challenge. Confuse. And if nothing between these covers does the business for you... write your own.

Rikki Beadle-Blair

Lit Thoughts

When people say minority or – that much abused word – 'diverse', they usually mean black. But there's more to minority than that.

When we reached out for contributions for and from under-represented ethnicities, a thrilling array of writers responded, which for me was a dream come true. I've written a lot of scripts. I've created a lot of characters of countless different cultures, ethnicities, classes and backgrounds. I love immersing myself in the widest range of voices, rhythms, cadences and nuances. It's been a mission of mine to find voices and faces less heard and seen, and put them on the stage, radio and screen. But the human spectrum is infinite and life is definitely finite. That's why if I meet you and you tell me your stories or talk about people you grew up with, work with, compete with, I'll probably ask you: Do you write? 'Cause even better than writing widely, is reading widely. And mentoring the writers in this book has been an educational bonanza. British African-Caribbean-Mediterranean, East Asian-South Asian, Traveller, Scots, Irish, Welsh, Middle Eastern, Latin, Jewish voices and more. Yes, voices. Because this voice is made not just to be read, but to be performed. This book is a kaleidoscope of lesser-heard voices. It roars, purrs, whispers, sighs, weeps and laughs out loud.

There's a world of representation in this book. You may find a bullseye in these pages written by someone who comes from a family like yours. You may find a piece in here that's written by or for a totally different ethnicity that speaks your truth. Borrow, adapt it. Make it yours. We find ourselves in one another. That's what art does. Whatever colour or shade you are, there's something in here for you. We see you. We are you.

Rikki

Table of Contents

079ME
by Kiren Kebaili-Dwyer

TREY, 18. Tries to hide sad emotions behind humour. He's just watched a video on Instagram where he's been told he needs to talk more about how he feels, and that maybe he should start by talking to himself.

'/' indicates pause.

Trey   Right. So. /
Basically. Erm.
I've been told. To. Come. Here. *(Laughs)*
Erm. Told to, to… come here and have a conversation with you!

Nods at himself in the mirror for reassurance.

I'm meant to look you in the eye and tell you how I feel about you and how you're doing at the moment. And that's fucking mad because I don't often talk to you. Definitely not as much as I should. I'm scared. /

I'm scared of what that might start up here *(indicates head)* and that's fucked because I've needed to talk to you for a long time.
Erm.
Let's just say I forgot your number. *(Laugh)*
Oop, found it. *(Laugh)*
Erm, connection's been a little bit wobbly recently.

Laughs, settles and recomposes.

You.

Are.

Important.

And as hard as the viruses in this world try to infect you, just keep reminding yourself that you are important, and you are strong. But sometimes, it's okay to – cry. To, show emotion. It's okay to be hurt by those really little things that just keep piling up.

Laughs.

Because that's what it's like being mixed-race in London. it's crawling with all these countless tiny little viruses that aren't that powerful by themselves, but they float around in the air like dust, barely visible – you can't see them invading through your eyes and your ears and you don't feel them until it's too late, until they all pile up inside your head and they clot... they clot in the brain. And I know this has started happening to you because you are already questioning every encounter, in fear of an attack.

Every – odd look.

Every – cross of a pavement.

Every failure. Every success. Every time that a girl says, 'Oh, you're buff'. Every. Time. They – get your order wrong at Costa or some shit. Every time.

'Was that because of the colour of my skin?'

You can't help but let that question come to your head and that's so fucked. But it's alright, its gunna be alright, yeah. Because I'm not gunna let you be treated like that anymore. So /

Next time. You. You come to me, yeah. Because if we don't catch those viruses, then that clot will grow and cause a cancer of the mind. Which will also grow until it consumes you and you become bitter and angry and even more depressed than you are now. Because I see it in your eyes, I can see that they've already got to work, they're already spreading, and I don't wanna lose you. so /

So…

Save the number, yeah.

Chin up. This was good. You did well. Talking to me.

Laughs.

To… yourself…

Laughs.

You've got the number saved now, so call yourself, whenever, pop it on speed dial or something.

Laughs.

Just keep talking to me, yeah.

Please.

I just kinda liked it, that's all… it was nice and I'm not saying I wanna, you know, make this official or anything… but yeah… just…

079me, init.

142 days
by Nina Cassells

Ruby Sometimes I look at you and I just feel sick. Honestly I do. When I'm with you – and I'm saying this because I love you – I feel like I'm in a little dinghy pitching and rolling across the ocean and my stomach wants to throw up all its contents. Your sadness makes me physically ill. So, can you really blame me for distancing myself? I'm not a horrible person but there's no joy in our friendship anymore, and I don't want to be around someone who doesn't get out of bed. I want to live. Fuck, when was the last time you lived? The last time you danced? When was the last time you filled a plastic bottle with vodka and downed it outside a club? When was the last time you stuck pills down your bra? When was the last time you even washed? I'm saying this all as a friend, because I sincerely want you to be that girl again.
And because you smell.

It feels like you're losing yourself and it makes me sad. I don't like being sad. A part of me suspects you do.

Do you want to, like, say something or –?

'Cause I can't read your mind, you know. I'm not a therapist. I don't know how. There's no formal education that prepares you for the responsibility of being a friend. I can't look after you.

It takes all of my strength to look after myself.

I used to know this girl. She didn't get out of bed for 142 days. It was like her skin was glued to the sheets. Time didn't matter. It was endless. It, like, stretched over her and consumed everything she loved, until eating felt like a chore and talking like a form of exercise. She thought, 'I could go on in this life without saying a word and no one would notice. Not a single person. And maybe if I concentrate hard enough, if I silence my thoughts and try really really hard not to take this next breath… I could disappear altogether. How nice would that be?'

I'm scared for you, is what I'm trying to say. The mind's a powerful thing when it wants to be. I've seen it. I've felt it. I promised myself I wouldn't be that girl anymore. But when I'm with you, all I can see is her.

It's an ugly thing to look at.

Anyway, I guess that explains why I haven't been around much.

I also find you incredibly boring. So there's that too.

Ackee and Saltfish
by Stephanie Josephs

Gabriella   Enough. I've had enough, of not being enough. When I was younger, at breakfast I would feel invincible, full snap, crackle and pop. Knew my worth, felt my own words and was full of beans, the kind you put on the hopscotch to mark the number where you're gonna jump. Jelly, kidney, butter, black-eyed beans means feeling like you know where you're from. Rooted. Sprouted. A half-baked education left me craving, hungry for a full menu of my history because some things just did not sit right with me. Yes, I had heard occasionally of bananas and plantations but nothing of the yams and stews and whole foods. Maybe a likkle rice and peas, but for me it became too clear that when it comes to making peas gungo, broad, snap, green, I'd need to seed my way out of this state of inequality where I'm judged not by my authentic recipe, passed down through generations, but by the label's presentation before you even get to try a taste.

'How much, luv?'

That'll be £5.95 thank you.

'You got some salt and vinegar for my cod and chips?'

6

Condiments are at the end of the counter. Help yourself.

'How 'bout you give us a smile? Might never happen...'

(Not smiling) Have a good evening.

Yes, currently I'm feeling salty as the ackee and saltfish of my nation as well as sweet like the juicy plantain, but these flavours I can't savour when, time and time again, I'm convinced I'm not enough. Is it something I learnt – that every morsel had to be earnt? And I feel like a jerk for internalising, believing the lies, because I ain't no chicken. But the way people see me is hitting different, and it's like inside I know I've got spice, I've got tasty fire, hot like scotch bonnet, wanna put my stamp 'pon it – but I still don't feel like I'm enough. I attempt to heal my soul with ital feeding from the earth to nourish myself. It's vital because rather than belly full I just feel...

...kind of empty.

Alien Baby
by Li Sa Choo

Jia Lin You used to have this look. Simultaneously rolling
your eyes, clicking your tongue and shaking your
head at me. The holy trinity of disapproval, I called
it. It used to make my blood boil but it's sort of
funny now cos I find myself doing the exact same
thing to Leo. Constantly. I just can't relate to him,
this child, this alien *thing* that I apparently gave
birth to. Sometimes I fantasise that his real family
will teleport into my kitchen, apologise for the
inconvenience, and finally relieve me of this curse
forever. But instead, I roll my eyes, I click my tongue
and I shake my head at him. Of course that usually
initiates a screaming tantrum which I then willingly
participate in – who can out-scream who? Four-
year-old child or twenty-six-year old Mum?
Hilarious. Maddening. Pathetic.
But then I compare it to what you had to deal with,
and I just feel ashamed. Working as a midwife with
the three of us on the go, and here I am having a
screaming match with a child who can't be left
unattended with a bowl of chopped apple.

I really thought you were trying to control me,
growing up. Thought you were disappointed cos I
wasn't this inhuman, perfect *robot* churning out
GCSE after GCSE as soon as I emerged from the
birth canal. Now I realise, if you were disappointed

it was because I was just an all-round terrible human being. Stupid girl. Skipping school, stealing from you, disappearing for weeks on end, gallivanting around like I didn't have people who cared about me.

But now I can see you for who you are. Arriving in this awful country at nineteen with just a suitcase and the promise of a nursing job at some shitty London hospital. All those years spent delivering babies who would grow up to yell 'chink' at your own children on the street. Cleaning up people's shit, being screamed at. And I gave you nothing in return, just more of the same.

You would be so sad to see how everything turned out. But God, I'd give anything to see the holy trinity now. I admit it. I miss you. I wish you were still around to tut and sigh at me, to tell me how wrong I'm doing everything.

I'd give anything for that.

I might even take your advice.

Aloo Qeema
by Sachal Khan

RAJA is a teenage migrant. Racism from peers and teachers, a failure to identify with parts of his own culture, and a festering alienation have changed his relationship with food for the worse. Hiding his disordered eating from his chaotic and nosy family has been hard, but he reckons just scraping under their radars is good enough.

When Ramzan comes around and the whole family starts fasting, Raja begins to realise the toll it is taking, and that something needs to change.

Bedroom. Raja enters holding a plateful of food, and kicks the door shut behind him.

Raja   I'll eat at the table tomorrow, Baba, *qasam*! Tomorrow!

Slumps to the floor.

So where am I gonna hide you this time? Can't be the bins again, not for the fifth time. Ammi has to find you eventually. 'You think I cook these for the bin men?' I could bag you up and donate you or something. *(To his plate)* You got any ideas?

The food sits quietly.

Yeah, what do you know, you're just meat and bread. All you wanna do is take up space. I wish I could just fucking eat you. But we both know I'm not a curry muncher anymore.

Gets up and looks at himself in the mirror.

The first time someone called me a curry muncher I had no idea what he meant. The tenth time someone called me a dirty Paki, the word stopped being strange… and just made me feel sad. By the time I lost count of the Pakis, terrorists, the dune coons and rag heads, I was too hungry to notice. Too busy trying to make myself disappear.

Maybe I was always meant to be a white kid, and all the white kids know it, and that's why they hate me. They hate that they can't change something that's already final.

What do you think? Could Raj be a Rob?

The food sits quietly.

Didn't think so.

Baba used to say I eat like a true Punjabi. 'Every breakfast is a buffet!' Lying on the sofa with a full belly, feeling like a king.

(Tracing his stomach on the mirror.) Some fucking Punjabi you are now. Stupid. Starving won't make your skin any whiter. You're stuck in this *badshakal* body forever.

Somewhere, there's a planet with a white Raja on it. I wonder what he's like.

Throws himself onto the bed.

He smells like fish and chips and Lynx, and... whatever else white boys smell of. No one tells him to fuck off and play cricket when he picks up a football. He eats baked beans instead of *aloo qeema* and pigs out on Sunday brunch.

I guess there's also a planet with a Raja on it who eats like a Punjabi. He thanks Ammi for his meals. He collapses on the sofa next to Baba and they hold their swollen tummies together and complain about their *rosa*s for the rest of the day.

His cheeks are full and beautiful. He doesn't count his calories down to every last cup of *chai*.

Yeah. Yeah, he fucking loves *aloo qeema*. And he doesn't care about being a curry muncher or a Paki. He tells every one of those *chutiyas* to get fucked.

I mean, I see that Raja every day. When I'm out there, they don't know the difference between him and me. He's there at *sehri*, telling Ammi that food was delicious. He keeps his *rosa* and breaks it together with the family.

He's right here, so close I can see him. I could touch him.

If I could be that Raja, just for a minute.

I could... stay at the table a little longer next *sehri*. When I feel like running away, just sit tight. Maybe even take a bite. And enjoy what Ammi cooks for me. Maybe even savour it.

(To his plate:) What do you think? — fuck that, you're just meat and bread.

Picks up his plate and starts scraping food into his deskside bin.

Tomorrow. I'll stay a minute longer, tomorrow. *Qasam se*, I will.

GLOSSARY

Aloo qeema – potato and mince meat dish, served with rice or roti (flatbread)
Ammi and *Baba* – mum and dad
Badshakal – ugly/misshapen
Chutiya – vulgarity similar to 'cunt'
Rosa – fasts kept during Ramzan
Sehri and *iftar* – meals before and after breaking fast, respectively
Qasam/Qasam se – 'I swear!'

As I Go Along
by Lekhani Chirwa

JADE: Mixed-race Northerner, age 22-28.

Jade   I've got so many questions, I actually don't know
where to start.

It would probably be too overwhelming. To *finally*
be able to interrogate my identity and maybe finally
understand things better. Like why you never
taught me how to do my own hair. Maybe it was
too hard? Well, I can tell you now, it *is* hard. It's a
bloody mission. *(Little laugh.)* But I worked it out
eventually. As you can see.

Or why you moved us all the way up here when we
could've just stayed in London. What was it that
drove you to leave somewhere where things might
'ave been easier for us? Where I would 'ave grown
up to be a different person entirely – yeah, you
would've been different too, but would that 'ave
been so bad?

Maybe I could find out why I had to live my life as
an outsider and how you never once picked up on
that. How come there weren't one single conversation about anything to do with the fact that I'm half
black? How you managed to act like it wasn't even a
thing. Why there's a whole side to me that I know
nothing about, and why you won't even tell me

where Dad's from. Yeah, yeah, you say you don't know, but quite frankly that's not fucking good enough.

Look, I'm sorry. I know I've not been very kind as of late. It's been so shit. Seeing you like this. Knowing I should of been there for you regardless. But I've been working through a whole lifetime of shit. I look back on those times when I'd experience racism and I'd come crying to tell you and you'd just tell me to ignore it, pay them no mind and shut down the conversation. And I'm like, well, now the shoe's on the other foot and you need me, so screw you.

I know that's ungrateful. I know you have given me so much. A life, for a start. And I appreciate the experiences and opportunities you managed to give me, I do. But I have to be honest with you, you neglected to teach me about who I was, and I've been lost my entire life. Making it all up as I go along. Forever trying to work out ways to assimilate. You won't ever fucking understand what that even means. Bless you. But you know one thing I've finally actually sorted out? Where I'm from. I took one of those DNA tests. I worked it out on my own. So yeah, thanks for nothing, Sharon.

...Mum.

How did you meet my dad? Did your family accept him or did they threaten to disown you? Is that why they treat me different?

So many questions that will never be answered.
'Cause now you can't even communicate with
me properly, you get too emotional because of
your condition. Finally an excuse for you being so
dismissive. And that's a real tragedy.

Babylon Ballet
by Stephanie Tykeya (Stephanie T. Clarke)

ANAYA ISOLYN SINCLAIR, dancer, age 18-35. Accent: Jamaican.
Location: Judges' panel room. Anaya begins her routine.

Anaya *(British teacher accent)* '1, 2, 3, 4. Inhale, exhale. Hold your tummy in, Anya. I said hold your tummy in, Anya, do not let them know you're starving. 1, 2, 3, 4, do not let them know your feet hurt.'

Out of breath, Anaya holds a pose.

'Your kind does not belong here. You hear me: no large coloured women.'

Defeated, she falls to the floor.

My name is Anaya. Not *(mimics teacher)* 'Anya'.

9 months walking on my own and dancing in my cradle.

Age 2 landing the perfect pirouette.

Age 6 spoken of as a dancing prodigy.

Age 8 I nearly lost my toe playing with the gully boys. Nanny nearly gave me the beating of my life; I was supposed to be buying chicken foot for her at Linstead Market.

Age 14, the perfect arabesque.

Age 16 moved to the UK with my Moomy Yonie and Granny Ida May.

I was one of the best, but they never treated me

like that. Some days my shoes were taken out my locker, sometimes they spat in my face and every time I made a report it was always

(British clerk) 'Yes Ms Sinclair, we will look into this matter, you know the Dance Academy does not condone any racial discrimination, we stand in solidarity with the Black community.'

Funny, because there were only four of us, so who was they really standing with? Other students and I started protesting. Times were getting harder, the oppressor was getting stronger and I started to share my truth about the government. The academy did not like that. Discrimination, bad indoctrination. We did not have equal pay, the segregation got worse. Britain promised us a new life of opportunity to build but instead we got no papers, in fact they got rid of our documents.

One day I was at a protest in Parliament Square. I met this mad gyal, Sally. 'Sickhead Sally' I called her. She said, *(Cockney accent)* 'You know what Nya, let's just blow them all up.'

I said, 'Pardon me?'

'You heard me right. I mean, they ain't going to stop, they ain't going to one day wake and decide not to oppress, that would mean they lose their power. They ain't going to do that. Hear me out. I got an uncle who's got a nephew who's got a friend that's got a brother who knows their business about bombs. We can just get rid of them, Nya. You gotta

be on some Malcom X business: "any means neces-
sary". Respect is earned. It's territorial.'

They locked up Sickhead Sally for terrorist plots
soon   after, I never heard from her again.

She was right, though; protests were our only
answer. The oppressor speaks in money. Crash the
economy then they will listen.

Granny said, 'If you waan gud yuh nose haffi run.
Keep on dancing, baby. Keep on singing, baby.'

(Sings) 'Police and thieves in the street, fighting the
nation with their guns and ammunitions. Police and
thieves in the street, oh yeah scaring the nation
with their guns and ammunitions.'

Bruised and torn I feel like a rag doll. I wish I could
cut out my eye, pull it from the socket so I could
unsee some of the thing I have seen in this life. If
we turn a blind eye, play the part, remain silent,
then we can navigate easier, right. *(Laughs.)*
Crosses, I will not stay silent no more. We will not
stay silent no more.

The principle said they had to let me go, revoking
my scholarship. I knew it was because I spoke about
the injustices. My dream came crashing down.
Granny said   it is time to pack up.

Pack up! But we've come this far, Granny, pack up?
No, I refuse. We cannot let them win. I mashed up
the place. I did not leave the academy without a
fight. As Leviticus 24, verse 19 says, 'A breach for a

breach, eye for eye, tooth for tooth.'

Pauses.

> I will not stop; I will not stop fighting. Nor will I take the colonisers' drugs, to let you discard me like rubbish. I refuse to stop. Are you listening? I said are you listening?

Panting for breath, Anaya restarts her dance routine.

> 1, 2, 3, 4, Learie Constantine. 1, 2, 3, 4, Stuart Hall. 1, 2, 3, 4, Claudia Jones. 1, 2, 3, 4, Olive Morris. 1, 2, 3, 4, Aletheia Jones-LeCointe. All paving the way for Black power and equality. We will never stop. I am Anaya Sinclair, in Granny's eyes Black Majority Ballerina, in the media's eyes a Black Radicalist, in the Academy's eyes an angry Black woman. So tell me, what am I in your eyes?

> Yes, there's blood on my hands, but there's blood on your hands too: you contribute to the suffering.

> I guess we're all guilty.

Anaya closes her eyes.

> Deuteronomy 20, verse 1: 'When you go out to war against your enemies, and see horses and chariots and an army larger than your own, you shall not be afraid of them, for the Lord your God is with you, who brought you up out of the land of Egypt.'

> Your chains no longer hold me. I will never stop fighting. I will never stop dancing. This legacy, the Black legacy, my legacy, it will never stop.

Exits. Blackout.

Better Out Than In
by Kami Gakuru

Lights up on ISABELLE, preening herself in front of a body-length frame she uses as a mirror.

Isabelle   Oh hey! My name is Isabelle, I'll be your entertainer this evening, lucky you.

She squeezes her body through the frame, walks towards the audience. Waits for a response.

Hmm, no applause at that... okay, that's fine. It's a choice. I should tell you that I'm here not because I want or need your validation, but because *I* have a gift. If I don't grace the stage with my presence, who else will shine through the clouds of your dreary lives and give you hope for a better tomorrow?

Brightly laughs until the sound chokes in her throat.

I haven't been in a room this hostile since Shropshire... Well, of course I'll tell you what happened! See, I'd got a blowout on a hot day and was sweating my edges into a frizz. Well, in the supermarket a lady said to me that she just loved the texture of my hair, and I replied that I loved the colour of her blood as I stabbed her to death. What's that saying? Better out than in? At least I was able to give out event flyers while I had everyone's attention. Would've have been a packed out show, I'm sure.

Isabelle eyes up the audience.

Oh, don't look at me like that. She knew that my hair wasn't what it should have been. She *knew* I was nervous about performing my set in 'Caucasian Land' that night. She was *mocking* me. She knew my insides so I took a look at hers. No harm, no foul. Well... *some* harm.

Pauses to think.

Her broken body was kind of foul. She looked so beaten, so... foreign. Like she was never a person. Just a doll.

(Reminiscing.) You know when you're little and you get a new doll with long hair? That amazing feeling you get when you cut and chop all that lovely hair off... Then that stab of pain when you realise it's not pretty enough to be a nice dolly anymore. It's only good for reminding you what dolls shouldn't be. No one actually wants *that* doll.

Changes to a self-congratulatory tone.

So I killed most of the witnesses too. Spared them the memories.

Smiles, satisfied, charming.

Is everyone having an amazing night so far?!

Black Girl Struggles
by Jessikah Wilson

Violet   Struggle 57 – Hair.
Monday, you'll wake up with a fully cooperating
'fro, extra bouncy. Come Tuesday, you're looking
like Barkhad Abdi from *Captain Phillips*. 'Look at me,
look at me. I'm the captain now.'
You couldn't imagine the amount of people that just
come up to me and touch my hair.
Sorry Becky, can you take a second to understand
that this *(gestures to self)* is not a petting zoo?
So what if I've got braids this week? So what if my
hair grew 22 inches overnight and turned bright
red? You could never.

Struggle 72 – Demeanour.

(Sings – [busy signal: unknown number])

'Mi arx, ooz callin' me from a unknown number? Mi
nuh answer no unknown number – Is who dat?'

(Instant code-switch to R.P.) 'Oh, hello, sir… Yes,
this is she.'

Struggle 81 – Judgement.
Being condemned as a prostitute for wearing ripped
jeans to church. Being classed as a nun for hiding
your cleavage on nights out. Seeing Aunty Joy's
daughter shooting you daggers at church 'cause you
let your weave down and bruk'd up your back at 11

p.m. on Saturday but came to sing 'Jesus na you be Oga' at 12 p.m. on a Sunday.
The culture-clash of infused religion and social acceptance.

Struggle 96 – Skin.
I can't just wake up, splash water on my face and call it a day, you know!
I have to have a daily debate about leaving the house un-creamed. Sorry – 'un-moisturised'.
If I don't, my black friends will rip me to shreds for being ashy, but if I do, my white friends will say I look oily. Or greasy.

It's actually peak because you can cream as much as you like, but by time the front door shuts – Elbows? Ashy. Knees? Ashy. That little hymen between your thumb and index? Hella ashy!
I usually compromise and cream the visible parts of my body. Then I started drama school and my feet were looking like some next sandy, misty, foggy... Pshh! Which brings me to...

Struggle 119 – Education.
I think I blocked out most of my secondary school black girl struggles due to trauma.
Drama school though, as a black, mostly straight female – oh so high on my struggle list.
The first time our whole year was together and I realised I was the only black person.
Don't even wanna talk about the first time the

whole school was together. It was like, 'Where's Wal- oh, there he is.'

My first role, I was cast as Tituba in *The Crucible* – classic. Smashed it.

Next a news reporter. Thought I'd play her as a troubled single mother, battling addiction, edgy backstory and all that, but no.

'You know what would really work for you? Play her as a preacher woman.' Excuse me? 'You know! Like... Whoopi Goldberg! You know, *Sister Act*, right?'

Struggle Infinity – Survival.

Constantly tiptoeing along the invisible line between being unapologetically black and female, and the gracious team player. All while wrestling with the restraints of society and culture, family, friends, people's expectations vs my expectations. Staying sane and focused in a world that's designed to force us to live in a tiny little box in the corner of our feelings, hoping to avoid being labelled as the aggressive, angry black girl.

That is struggle number one.

Blessings
by Lucia Deyi

Henan, China, 1978.

Yi Shi   Ba, Ma. I've been thinking for some time and I've decided to ask the Shaolin monks to take me up as their disciple.

I've been contemplating the words you used to read to me every night, Ba, from the Lotus Sutra:

'Men in all the world have forsaken
Their jewel-covered sedans
Their families and wives,
To seek for answers on the path
And lay on the robes of the law.'

I've been torturing myself over these words. How can I leave my family behind when I owe my parents everything? There wasn't a night that I studied into the early morning hours in which I didn't think about the verses of that sutra, Ba. And even before I graduated high school there were so many moments: when grandfather died; the time those kids drowned the tiny newborn kittens; or that day I almost died walking home from town that winter... I always remembered your voice and those verses, Ba, through nights and mornings and summer and snow.

I'm not certain if I'll ever understand everything. Or

even anything. It's a mystery how the words of those verses have absorbed every thought and every feeling, but they have. And now I can't imagine my life without those words in my mind.

Believe me, I am more than grateful.
What you have given so generously, humbles me.
But I don't believe in this cruel civilisation's cold future promise.
I don't believe in working for happiness as long as we walk the beaten path, stay loyal to the state, marry and continue creating families without asking questions, over and over again.
What are we to them? Simple folk. Dirty, uncultured farmers
For fine city folk to make fun of.
Why should I give them one more body to walk over?
One more idiot from the countryside to make empty promises to?
No. Never.
I'd rather take my own life than let it be stolen.

Pause.

There's something within me that yearns to become quiet
Refuses to take part in this never-ending
Hope-making and ladder climbing.
This is not my world, Ba. I want to live with other monks
And understand the world through teachings.

I need to be amongst those who don't pretend
To know anything in the world, a world free
Of rivalry and competition.
The world described in the texts you taught me, Ba!
In which men give their lives for answers.

I know this is a shock, but please understand that
my decision to become a monk is not an attack on
our family.
If anything it is a tribute to you both and all you
have taught me.
And the man you have made me.
And I thank you.

Beat.

Can you give me your blessings?

BLICK
by Kadiesha Belgrave

IMMY: Intellectual Black Female.

Immy   Do you remember them girls, the ones that the guys you had crushes on cared to get to know at secondary 'cause THEY were the BUFFTINGS, so you yourself would steer clear of the people that labelled them the bufftings in order for you not to be called a blick ting.

And its mad 'cause, even though you were proper embarrassed, you would try and convince yourself that they weren't talking about you, 'cause you weren't no blick ting. 'Cause if you were that black, who would want you? I remember being thirteen years old, sitting in the library with the girls that were lighter than me, and listening to insults from their admirers all around us.

'Err she's blick fam', 'nah nah if she ain't got the light skin, green eyes and curly hair then take her away innit', 'ey team light skin innit I don't want no blick ting'…

And you know, the funny thing about it was that it weren't the white kids making me feel a way about my melanin, it was you lot. The mandem who didn't wanna stick up for their galdem. Meanwhile I tried to fix it – Lord knows I tried to fix it – I relaxed my hair and I prayed. *(Trying to make a joke out of it.)*

Imagine praying to God 'cause you didn't wanna wear His gift anymore!

I didn't wanna be the butt of the joke, I wanted to be inside that circle making the jokes. It was almost like there was a barricaded door in between the middle of us and I was I knocking at it, then banging at it, and then screaming against it till I couldn't. And then I started to deny myself wanting to be let in, and it seemed that when I did I was the traitor – or the 'Oreo' or the 'coconut'. Always the loser, never the winner.

Uncomfortable silence.

Don't get me wrong. I remember good things. Like sitting in between my mum's legs watching *Sister Act 2* whilst she did my hair... Watching Lauryn Hill rap with her '90s braids and her locs and the black guys actually... wanting her – you know, like wanted to know who SHE was... Kind of like what you do to the lighter girls now. *(Small smile.)* Her skin looked so soft, like chocolate or something... you know I got my first set of braids 'cause of her *(laughing)* and I remember walking around with my long ass hair, ready to take on any dickhead who wanted to chat about what I looked like... *(Smile fades.)* You couldn't imagine how I felt after taking them out. Like Cinderella after midnight.

You know it fucks me up a little that suddenly us dark skin girls are getting the praise we deserved a long time ago 'cause Insta said it's okay now. And that people like you pretend that we were never the outsiders. Like you never said blick. And deep down I can't lie to you, Aaron – I still wait for you all to turn on us again. Just for existing.

Bread and Sugar
by Lantian Chen

LIANG FAN (梁帆), a single Asian mother in the United States.

Liang Fan (*Holding son's phone.*) Who's this boy – 'Elliot'? He's your friend, right? I don't understand why people these days like to pass around photos like this. Maybe I'm old... I don't know. You know once it's leaked on the internet it's gonna stay there forever, right? (*Shaking head.*) You will never become the President... What? Why can't you be one? You are an American citizen, remember that! You are just like everyone else. Why can't you... Where are you going?

Pursuing.

You listen right now! I'm your mother! Speaking in a language she learned as an adult in a foreign country twelve hours of flight away to give *you* a better life! I have raised you better than this. When I'm talking, or your grandparents, you have to stay there and...

Blocking son's way.

JASON!

Silence. Then gently,

You're... confused. It's okay. Sometimes we like to

play around with our friends and do some... experiments. It's *normal*. When I was growing up in China my friends and I even shared clothes to wear. Yes. Those dresses our mothers made from the materials saved from making the bedsheets. All those flower patterns... Of course, looking back now it's all very silly what went through our minds, but it's just... part of the process. Of growing up. It will pass. I promise.

You... like... him?

'Love him'?

But you can't. (*Beat.*) *We* can't. You know that.

Watching her son once again turn to leave –

Do you remember what you liked to eat when you were six? Yeah. I had to lock Nutella in the cupboard so you wouldn't destroy your teeth. One piano lesson, one slice of French toast. Just a single piece of bread and sugar could make you so *happy*. So happy... I don't know why now... you are like... a person I don't know anymore. Neighbours keep saying how smart you are, how proud I must be. I... I have to *smile*, and answer with some stupid jokes because I don't know what to say! Since you left for Harvard – the college I've worked for fifteen hours every single day to put you into – you've never talked to me about anything! And now... Do you really think you can call whatever you are doing with that Elliot boy as... what, 'love'? (*Laughs.*) Let me tell you, there's only one kind of *love* you can trust in this whole world, and that comes from *me*... Why do you have to do this to me? How are you going to *make babies* with that little monster?? Your penis is not going into a womb – it goes into SHIT!

Hurls the phone. Beat. Breathes.

So that's why you didn't come home for Thanksgiving? Him?... 'I gotta stay on campus ma. You don't know how stressful the finals are'... so you could eat fucking turkey with *his family*?

Raises a hand to her son. Slaps her own face. Bursts into tears.

I should've... I should've... I should've checked in with other parents more often... to see how you were doing at school. I should've moved to Boston with you so you could come home every night. I should have checked your phone. Should have helped you find a good girl and decent friends. I should've been there when you needed me the most... I should never have come to this country. I should've stayed with your father...

Calms down... With a little smile, looking directly into his eyes –

I should've had that abortion.

Calmest Voice
by Isabelle Kabban

Thea: Sometimes I want to smash his face in with a lamp.

I think about being upstairs and hearing him slamming doors around the house. Hearing him cough. Hearing him go into my mum's room. Hearing his hushed voice. Hearing him laugh. Hearing him make a joke for the hundredth time that is never fucking funny. Hearing him speak on the phone to god knows who in the middle of the night. And I know I cannot go back there.

There was this one time, stop me if I've already told you this. I was crying because he'd done something that made me and my mum really angry, right, and when I get angry I just cry. And he got his phone out and started filming me cry. He was laughing and he told me he would watch the video later with his girlfriend. His laugh was so fucking shrill and piercing. And breathy. I could see the spit in his mouth. All over his teeth. He had this vicious energy around him, you could almost see it.

I imagine picking up the big living room lamp and smashing his face in. Not so he dies or anything. I don't want him to die. But just hurt him enough so that he disappears for a bit. So it punishes him. Shocks him.

And the thing is, I feel like a bit of an idiot. I feel like an idiot that I didn't realise sooner how fucked up that was. That my brother could do that, you know. And I wish that rather than crying and screaming and getting 'hysterical' and giving him that satisfaction I had said to him in the calmest voice, 'Laugh at me if it makes you feel better, Calum. You can record me if you want, because the truth is I have literally given up caring. I'm ten years younger than you and far braver than you will ever be. I'm glad you can laugh. But you know I have more fire and drive and strength and resilience and power inside me than you will ever possess in your whole entire fucking life. You pathetic man.'

But I don't say that.

Come Away

by Sanjay Lago

Vikram   I know I shouldnae have woke you up in the
middle of the night, Billy, but I am losing ma fucking
mind. Let's go fetch Rita and come away from this
place. We can go to London or Brighton. You said it
yourself the other day, that you wanted a fresh
start.

NAW! Dinnae tell me to calm doon. I am calm, if a
bit tipsy, but I ken what I am talking about.

(Tearfully.) Please, you're ma best friends. I can't go
on further. I've packed my bags and left a note, I
want to break free like Freddie. I want to scream
and shout, like Britney, and let it all out. And you
are ma only hope.

I had tay dae it! I cannae live with being a letdown
of a son bringing shame on a desi household. You
saw how they reacted to ma sister, I was their last
and only hope. Not only are we Indian in Scotland,
we're Indian in Milngavie and I don't know if ma
parents could survive the shame. The pain.

The air has changed, mate. Ken whit ah mean? It's
like ma Nanu used to say when I was a child, he
would say, 'Whenever the air changes and you feel
the direction of the breeze shift to hit you head on,
you ken that change is coming. If rain comes with
that breeze then clear the path, as destruction

37

needs a path to go through before the roads are safe to walk down again.'

Luckily it ain't raining, even if it does look a bit dreich.

Help me oot mate. Look, I even have money, I took ma savings all with me. Yes, I know the task is hoachin' of things going wrong.

Am NO being a bampot!

I was yesterday having a shower and bursts in ma mother. Luckily I had a sponge to cover ma modesty, the one I got at Universal Studios in the shape of an ice-lolly. Not the biggest but it worked. And she's shouting over the shower curtain that there were a long line of bonnie lassies queuing up for me, waiting to join the Milngavie Punjabi house. I tried to laugh, and she reaches and skelps me right oor the heid.

She's right. It's no funny at all. I'm another one who's gonna break her heart. She is dying for another white horse in this street. But I dinnae ken if I can handle another two weeks of crazy auntyji's and unclejis screaming at me. Or any of what comes after.

And you ken what, I may not be that son. I may not be the stereotypical desi man. But at the end of the day I am human and just want to be loved for who I am.

Gives a small laugh to himself.

You'd think they would know already though. I mean, at the Gurdwara I always wanted to take a chooni instead of a ramal to cover ma head. I loved dancing like Madhuri or Kareena. Sorry – they're actresses from Bollywood. Madhuri did the dance to the dance I choreographed for in the high school Third Year show, remember?

Sounds like my own life is a Bollywood film, eh? I'm just wired tae the moon. Wee Vikram fae Milngavie. I hope one day to be someone's Kajol to their Shah Rukh Khan. It's true what they say, in life everywhere there is Khabi Khushi Khabi Gham. All we can hope for is that there is more happiness and less sorrow. Even if you are cut off from the rest of society in a land of not many rainbow desis around.

And if you help me, then I won't clype to yer maw about that baby you've been hiding in, where was it? Tobermory? That's it. I won't say to anyone where most of your money goes to at the end of the month.

Ah, fuck it, I'm even shite a blackmail. You know you're ma bestie and that I'll always have your back and I know you'll always help me with mine. I've got pieces and cans of ginger, mate! Let's run and get Rita, fuck this place off and start fresh, yeah?

Beat.

Yeah...? Yeah?? YEAAAAHHH! Fucking love you mate! Wait! *(Listens.)*
Is that the rain on?

You know what it means when the rain joins the breeze...

Glossary

Shouldnae – shouldn't
Ma – my
Naw – no
Dinnae – don't
Doon – down
Tay dae – to do
Cannae – can't
Desi – Indian
Milngavie (*Mull-Guy*) – a town in Scotland
Chooni (*choo-knee*) – the scarf with a salwaar kameez
Ramal – head covering used in religious places
Ay – a
Ken – know
Wired tae the moon – as in 'the lights are on but no one is home'
Wee – small
Fae – from
Clype – a tell-tale
yer maw – your mum

Ken whit ah mean? – know what I mean?
Dreich – wet/grey
Bonnie lassies – good-looking girls
Heid (heed) – head
Hoachin' – full of
Ginger – a can of fizzy juice
Pieces – sandwiches
Right oor – right over
Nanu – Grandad

Conversations with Spike and Samuel
by Stephanie Stevens

Temi   I'm not mad. I'm not.

I share your pain… I feel it. I feel for you.

I know that you are constantly overlooked and at the same time lectured.

Maybe the film wasn't that GOOD, Spike.

If you make GOOD movies, Sam, then people will watch them and vote for them and you'll win awards.

Respect, Mr Lee, *Do The Right Thing* was iconic. A masterpiece of contemporary cinema, it depicts so much that our society keeps circling back to and has never been more relevant. And you, Samuel-L-'Bitch Be Cool'-Jackson, you've been in at least 133 films, you read kids' bedtime stories and make them sound like action films, most guys want to be like you, as badass as you. I will never deny how important you both are.

That's why it wounds so deep, to hear you say Black Brits are cheaper.

'Cheaper.'

Why it kills to hear your characters say Black Brits have Stockholm Syndrome, that we're in love with our white captors.

Do you think our ancestors were happily jumping into bed with their slavers and colonisers while your ancestors were the only ones suffering? Black history is not just American history. Your audience is not just Stateside. We are here worldwide, to connect to, to listen to, to learn about – learn from. We are part of the audience that gave you your platform and this is what you do with it?

Okay, now I am mad.

One actor getting one job dictated how you would respond to a whole community of people who support you, who are inspired by you, who love your work. You took a cheap jab. Like this is some kind of sport, like we're point-scoring. This is the Olympics, I'm going to say it, I'm really going to say it, this is the Oppression Olympics, and you seem to feel the need to beat us so that you can win.

But when you refuse to see us. We all lose.

Culture's got your tongue

by Yazmin Belo

Jolynne   Okay so look...

My mum shouting up to my room asking me to make her a cup of tea and I...

'Mek mi ah cup a tea nuh please.'

It's 8.30 and college starts at 9.

I tut aggressively, but only loud enough for me to hear. It's safer that way.

My clothes aren't ironed and I've tricked myself into believing I've got period pains

It justifies my sloth-like movement but isn't the reason I'm late today

Or why I am in this mess

Mum is.

Every day is always new

Duh!

However every day, yeah, also equates to discomfort.

Like having something stuck up your bum or up your nose unwarranted

The inability to talk up or out.

Mum shouts up again, 'And bring some biscuits wid it nuh please.'

She's taking the piss.

This time I internalise the tut, but invest in some extreme eye rolling.

It's safer that way

I tell myself I'm gliding down the stairs peacefully,
but really my face twiss up
I take each step as they come, frail but determined
like Mama Gertrude did before she got the stairlift
fitted.
Bless her.
She would have told me to speak up and talk out
She would of told me to tell Mum to bugger off
She would have told me to tell Mum I don't want to
be late to English Lit because I enjoy English Lit
Because maybe it's an escape
An escape from the ideologies and traditions that I
have been force fed.
It's about 8.40 – it's official, I'm not making it to
college on time, man
My anxiety grows but the tea won't make itself.
So I gather all my courage not to rebel and make my
way into the kitchen
I make the tea whilst humming Kate Bush – 'Wuth-
ering Heights'
It's a coping mechanism of mine. It works
And suddenly the thought of being half an hour late
to English Lit doesn't seem so bad.
I know we don't have any biscuits left because I ate
the last packet of bourbons
And not because I love bourbons, no, but because I
know she does
Still, I go through the motions of looking for the
nonexistent packet of biscuits

To keep the peace of course. Despite the war I'm feeling
Going through and shutting the cupboards with zeal
to show Mum I'm doing the job and putting in work
Why does it matter to me so much?

Beat.

'What ah tek so lang?!'
And all the bad words in my vernacular that I know
how to say are on the tip of my tongue
Instead I swallow it
'Won't be too long, Mum.'
But then I catch myself.
If I don't break this then who will?
Clarissa is 30 with two children and husband and
still wouldn't dare stand up to Mum.
I say a little prayer and beckon my ancestor to be
with me as I head into the living room to start a
revolution
I'm gonna tell my mother everything I haven't:
Mum!
Is this deliberate or do you just enjoy exercising
your authority with absolutely no cause?
You're numb so I'm numb, that's been your mantra
since Dad left and quite frankly I... I get it now
I get why he left.
You're unbearable. You know why I HATE missing
English Lit, why I hate being late or absent? Because
it means I become behind
Behind in class , behind in my assignments, behind

in LIFE and no, Mum, I can't ask a friend or a class-mate to keep me informed or updated because I have none because you don't let me out.

One day I want to apply to university, to study you know what. Yes, ENGLISH FLIPPING LIT, and I'm so sure I'll get into my first choice, Mum, you know why, because I am good at it.

And although there are number of things that will be used to set me back, I am determined to get through them in order to get away from you.

How?

After I finish university I will apply to be a teacher at one of the best schools in England, an English Lit teacher, and I'll rent an chic apartment somewhere fancy and have two cats and a ferret.

The only updates you'll have of me will be via Facebook and on weekends I'll spend the entire day with Dad, eating foods you never allowed me to have.

And no, I haven't mention marrying and moving in with a man because how do you expect me to love someone when I've never experienced love from you?

YOU BI...

Of course I don't say that, but as soon as I leave the living room I can feel my ancestors shaking their head in disapproval, screaming, 'SPEAK UP NUH GYAL, wah wrang wid yu?'

And in my frustration at being a wuss I pick up my bag and slam the front door with the energy I should have given to my mum, shattering the entirety of the glass.

I remain wrong and strong marching to the bus stop until I receive the text from Mum saying

'Don't budda come back to di yard until yu have di money to fix the door... yu lucky seh Gad is working in me, I wudda strangle yu.'

And now it's raining and I think I may have actually started my period. So yeah, that's why I'm here.

I need your help.

Dying in Your Shit
by Melissa Saint

CLARISSA confronts her mother on her deathbed.

Clarissa Yeah. That's right, I came. And what? I'm expected to clean up your shit? I'd rather watch you die in it. Maybe I should. I can only imagine how that would make you feel – Mrs Hoity-Toity, left to rot in her faeces. Hah! You always behaved like yours didn't stink. But trust me, it fucking reeks. There is no shit that smells as bad as yours.

Yes, I know... you always made a point of letting me know that you made me, I didn't make you – even here on your deathbed, it's all over your face how much it burns you just to look at me. That is what you'd be saying if your throat wasn't closing up and you could move your tongue with ease, right? What? Speak up! Cat got your tongue?

I can feel the sting across my face even now. I guess some things never change. You know, I thought Dad was wrong for leaving you. I hated him for so long until I properly understood. Maybe you were right, I am just like him. Clearly, he wasn't a fool either.

You never missed a chance to make me feel like I was hard to love – like I was unworthy, when the truth is, you're the one who's unlovable. That is why you're here, spending your last few hours alone and the only person that they can call is me.

And yet, knowing this, what you are, I still spent all of those years making myself small for you. Do you know what that does to a person? Do you know how venomous words can burrow their way into a person's brain like worms bury themselves in earth? Why'd you have to make it so hard for me to like you? Hmm? Why couldn't you – just once – listen to what I had to say? Was it jealousy? Resentment? Fear? Was I that much of a threat to you? Or is it because I look so much more like him than I could ever look like you?

Answer me.

You made our home a warzone. A child versus a grown-ass woman. You think that's fair? Well, go on... answer me before I rip this fucking tube right out of your nose!

Nothing?

I was a smart child, a good child – I didn't need your life lessons. I didn't need you to spit your filth in my face because all that did was break me into a thousand pieces. What I needed was a mother. Not a heartless bitch of an empty vessel that pushed me out.

I will never do what you did to me, to my children. Nor will I be as shit and as hypocritical as you. I will show them love and give them affection. I'm not quite sure how to, but I'll learn. And I'll do it, because no one knows better than me how much they'll need it.

You're going to die in your shit. And I'm going to watch you, not because I care, or because I'm hoping that even now you might find it somewhere in you to finally show me some... love.

Pulling it together. Refusing to break down.

But because you deserve to suffer. And I deserve to watch you. So, don't you worry, Mum, I'll be right here.

But you'll still be alone.

Eyes
by Adrian Tang

KEVIN, British Born Chinese. Freya is his partner; Josef is their son.

Kevin Josef! Come on, mate. You don't want to keep your mum waiting.

To Freya.

Alright? Did you see the video? Five goals!

To Josef.

And bagged a couple of assists, didn't you, son? Player of the match!

Why don't you show us your medal? It's in the car.

Listen, Freya, something happened yesterday. After the match. We were walking back to the car, I was saying how proud of him I am, and I was gonna treat him to Nando's, when one of the other dads on his team walks past and says, 'Man of the match! Maybe I need to get my son a pair of those funny-shaped eyes.' Like he thought it was a compliment or something.

I know I should have said something. But I didn't. Neither of us said much for the rest of the day. At lunch Josef just picked at his food. At the end he said something that broke my heart. He said –

Interrupted by Josef.

I'm not sure, son, I think it's in the car.

To Freya.

He was looking round at everyone's eyes. Then he said he didn't want to be Chinese anymore.

Pause. Breathes.

I think it's time he goes to Chinese school.

Hear me out. It's a couple of hours every Sunday morning during term time. I know you're not a morning person so I can pick him up from here when it's not my turn to have him. It's not a sneaky way of seeing him more or anything it's just… There'll be other kids like him there.

Interrupted by Josef.

Just find it in your bag!

To Freya.

Oh, and you never snap at anyone! *Our* son! Not just your son. He's my son too, Freya.

No no no no no. You get to take him back to Helsinki every year. He gets to eat all the Lohikeitto* he wants – which is great – meanwhile he can't even use chopsticks properly. I'm not blaming you, I'm blaming myself! I've been so busy making him proud to be British or European or Scandinavian or whatever when me of all people… I should have known one day he was going to hear some idiot say something like that.

Look, I already enrolled him, okay? Took him in this morning, he's registered and ready to start the new term. They say he should've started a year ago but that's okay, he's smart enough to catch up. He got his eyes from me but maybe if he learns Cantonese he'll understand.

If I'd known more. Paid more attention to where my folks were from. Where I'm from. Maybe I could have protected myself from all the bullshit.

Maybe I could have protected our son.

a traditional Finnish salmon chowder dish.

Faith
by Danielle Kassaraté

MICHELLE, early 20s, has just got off the bus outside Stratford station. She is on her way to Westfield but is stopped in her tracks when she is approached by the 'Megaphone Preacher'.

Michelle   Get your megaphone out of my face! Some of us just wanna go into Westfield and do a bit of shopping.

'YOU NEED TO BE SAVED; YOU ARE ALL LIVING IN SIN.' Shut up.

We should be saved from people like you.

Yes.

YOU.

Who told you to tell me how I should live my life?

Do not answer! It is a rhetorical question.

I am sick of it.

I am sick of the likes of you telling me how to feel, how to believe.

Listen, I will live my life how I want.

Pause.

OK. I know you think you mean well. My dad thought he meant well. I grew up in the church, I was there every Sunday, Monday, Tuesday, basically every day of the week.

I mean God rested on Sunday, why couldn't I?

Anyway, I spent my whole childhood in the church. In fact, I didn't even have a childhood, my best friend was Jesus. Don't get me wrong he is a great friend. I have a friend in Jesus.

But all my mates, were going out having fun, getting drunk

(Whispers) having sex

and I wasn't, I was too busy being a good girl. No, a good Christian.
So, I just ended up being vexed all the time everything pissed me off, because trying to be a good –

No. *Pretending* to be a 'good Christian' is *so* exhausting. I got to a point where I thought, fuck it. *(Catches herself quickly.)*
Sorry. Screw it.
So, I did.

I started doing things behind the minister's back, who is my dad by the way, did I mention that? Anyway, when the minister found out, my dad, what I'd been up to

Well, he beat the sin out of me.

Silence.

And I was at church the next day reading the bible with a dark bruise across my cheek.

Beat.

Everyone knew what he did. They didn't say nothing though. Just ignored it, because what I did was way worse.

I deserved it.
And in that moment, I saw the world for what it really is, and I saw the church for what it isn't.

All I did was go out raving a few times with friends, had a couple of Red Bull and vodkas. OK. Yeah. Maybe I was lipsing a couple of mens. OK. Yeah. Maybe I was doing a little bit more.

But I was living my life.

So that meant in the eyes of the lord – No, in the eyes of the Church – I was the devil. If that is the case, everyone is!

So, I never went back.

Pause.

OK, I'd be lying if I said I didn't miss it, the church, I do. I really do. I even miss how long it is. I never thought I'd say that, trust me. The atmosphere and the food. Yes, the food – listen, that after service food was everything, church makes you build up an appetite! Jesus broke the bread and after the service we were breaking them patties.

I miss a lot. Yeah.

I miss home. I think about my family all the time. My mum, even my sisters and they were really annoying.

Then there's my dad. Which is mad because after what he did to me, I still miss him so much it hurts.

Pause.

I will probably never talk to him again to be honest. Well, to them again. I don't want to change, and they will never come around so, yeah...

She starts to get emotional but quickly snaps out of it and focuses her attention back on the Megaphone Preacher.

I'm still glad I left, though!

Listen, nobody is perfect. Does that make us all sinners, or does it make us all human? Most of you all up in the church are not living the life you preach. Stop promoting your 'Christian' values and acting like you are holier-than-thou, because that you are not!

She goes to leave then comes back.

'Without faith it is impossible to please God.' Hebrews 11:6. Yes, I know the bible too.

Faith is what makes us whole! I have a lot of faith,

and a lot of love in my heart. I don't need to be saved to realise I have that.

That being said, if you will excuse me, I am going to go Primark to buy myself a nice likkle dress to show off some cleavage, and I will wake up tomorrow morning with a hangover and God will still love me.

Family

by Natasha Kathi-Chandra

Omala We don't do this in my culture. See a therapist. It's tricky in any culture, but it's seriously frowned upon in mine. We're full of oxymorons. Like you can drink but you can't smoke. You can have a boyfriend but you can't have sex before you're married. You can be an adult but can't make any adult decisions.

'Don't backtalk, and obey your elders.' – even if the elders are condescending, manipulative, abusive, two-faced, untrustworthy and, for want of a better word – bitchy.

Sorry. That's incredibly disrespectful.

Every Diwali, I had a duty to come to my grand-mother's house where the elders would be, full of condescending remarks about how badly brought up I was because I was living with my boyfriend, how rude I was because I had an opinion about why we shouldn't vote Conservative, and how selfish I was because I didn't visit my grandmother enough, especially now in her 'hour of need'.

My grandmother was the glue holding us together. I still have moments where something exciting happens, or I get good news, and I think, 'I should call Nani and tell her!' And then I notice the picture of her on my desk with a little electric candle burning in front of it, reminding me that she is gone. *(Looks up as if to the heavens, tears up.)* I hope my grandmother knew how much I loved her. Do you think she knew? Who knows.

Visibly upset, she clears her throat – attempts to lighten the mood.

December 11th 2019. Enfield Crematorium, a cold and grey day.

When we arrived with the coffin the estranged brother of my grandmother was the first of the guests to greet us in floods of tears. I'd never met him and he hadn't been in touch for nearly thirty years. My grandmother always pondered over that and asked why. I wish I could've told her it was probably because he molested my mother as a child but we don't do that. He was only an hour's drive away from where my grandmother lived, apparently, but at least he saw her now – even though it was in a shiny, brown coffin minutes before she was incinerated.

I'd never worn all white before but I think it worked for my skin tone. People had to stand at the back of the room we were doing the service in because all the 100 seats were taken. We are a well-known family in the community, my grandfather – who I never met – had made certain of that. All I could think about during the service was the host opening the gold envelope *(beginning to giggle)* and saying,

'And the Oscar for best fake family goes to...'

Laughs harder, then uncontrollably. Gathers herself.

I'm here because of them. Because it wasn't right.
All the years of being judged, being told I was
wrong. For having a voice. For having an opinion.
For trying to fight back.

I'm so angry.
I feel really hot.
Can we open a window?
I'm so angry.

Write it down? I've got so much to say and aren't
we nearly at time? Ten sentences? Yeah, I guess I
could do that.

Picks up pen and paper.

You're not going to ask me to read this out loud are
you?

The first word? It's 'You'.

The third sentence is, 'I am angry, hurt and broken
because of how you've treated me.'

The seventh sentence reads, 'This is not what a
family is.'

The first word of the ninth sentence? This is a weird
exercise! Sorry, this one's a bit rude – it says 'fuck'.
No, I'm not comfortable enough to read the whole
sentence.

And any three words from the last sentence…

Reads:

I've chosen them: 'not' and 'anymore'; and my third word is…

Family.

Finally reaches for the tissue box.

It's 'family'.

Fight
by Melissa Dewi

Mother   Okay then, go. Perhaps this is better for you. Children grow up. Children leave. So… leave. But don't forget that I tried. Really tried. Tried hard. This has not been easy for me: different country, still learning the language. One woman, Mrs Bishop, she was the *only* one who was never impatient with me. *Like this Sandra*, she would say. *It's pronounced like this*. She was tough with me. Tough and kind. Many will laugh, few will help you. So-called 'native speakers' here in Britain – No, I'm talking! So many of them are arrogant, yet capable of so little. And still, at work, when they see a foreign name or hear an accent, they think they're so much cleverer.

So, when you ask me why I haven't taught you 'our' language. Because you needed to speak perfect English to be taken seriously. And you are. No one is laughing at my child. Yet, you make laugh and make fun of me because I don't know how to hug, judge me for not being like other parents – those parents petting their soft delicate children saying, 'Oh, my poor baby, did you fall? Here's a kiss on your knee. See, everything is better now'… What life skills do you get from being praised for crying? What if the child gets raped next? A kiss and 'I love you' is not going to abort an unwanted baby, my son. People here say 'I love you' too much. 'I love you, I love you forever, I will love you in sickness and in health.' Three months later they'll sleep with other people; four months later: divorce. And all in perfect English! Love, my son, is not in language or words. Words are just sketches – stick pictures that call for too many interpretations...

Have I really wronged you so badly? For you to hate me so much, my child... when I have loved and fought for you with every ounce of strength in my body and spirit. I never meant to make your life harder. I just want you to live better. To grow up and be tall, so it's easier for you to buy trousers instead of shopping in the child section, like me. To love yourself as fiercely as I love you. That's all I ever wanted. For you to survive this country. And here you are. Saying you haven't survived me. Well then go. See how life treats you without what I've taught you. Without me.

Foreigner
by Julie Cheung-Inhin

ALICE – late 20s/early 30s, British-born with Sino-Mauritian heritage. This monologue would suit an actor of East Asian or South East Asian heritage.

Alice has applied to be an English teacher at Teach It!, an English school in China that employs TEFL teachers from the west for Chinese children of primary school age. This is her first class.

Alice　　Shall we get to know one other with a game? Let's go around the class introducing ourselves and saying what we enjoy! In English. Okay! Good Morning! I'm Miss Chong, your new English teacher, but you can call me Alice and I love noodles and dim sum and travelling and have always wanted to come here to see the Forbidden City!

(*Looking at student*) Hello... (*she tries to pronounce Zhi Ruo*) Jee Jur. Dzi jjj. Well... gosh, what a beautiful name! And what do you enjoy, Jeejurjij? Ooops! In English, remember!

Ah, um, yes, I am Chinese but I was born in Britain, so British Chinese! Now what do you... No, well I speak a few words of Hakka, actually, but I would love to learn Mandarin one day! Anyway, this is an English class and we're all speaking English! So... Who's next?

Do I love the Queen? Well, not really actually!

Yes, I do love tea. In England we drink it with milk.

Harry Styles? Oh! Well, I prefer BTS! Who likes BTS?

Okay, well, anyway….

Yes, Miss means I'm not married.

How old am I? In Britain we never ask that!

Right then…

No, I do not have a boyfriend.

Will I marry a Chinese man or a white man? Well, I don't know – maybe neith-

NO! White men do *not* –

Did I come here to find a husband?! Oh, my goodness, no –

Well, no, it's not that I prefer white men, or that I don't like Chinese men, it's that, um, it's about what's on the inside that matters, isn't it?

Wait – English, remember!

Now, no… we mustn't call anyone a banana.

Well, first of all, in England we never call Chinese people yellow – well, no one should, and it's even more offensive to say I'm white on the inside.

Well, of course I'm Chinese. But not all Chinese people speak – And my mother and father never spoke it round the house or...

Actually, I don't speak Chinese because I'm also Mauritian! I didn't mention it before because most Chinese people have never even heard of the place. Have you? You know what, never mind. Let's just ignore all that. Ignore that it's possible that people may have multiple heritages. Let's just focus on what I'm not – not Chinese enough, not British enough, not Mauritian enough. Not good enough. In England, can't walk down a street without 'Ni hao', can't say I'm British without 'But where are you really from?', can't say I'm Mauritian without 'But you don't look Mauritian to me!' So I come here. Sure, I knew there'd be some cultural shock, but I hoped that maybe, just maybe, I might be made to feel at home for once and somewhat normal. But no, I'm still a foreigner! Can't move without 'Why don't you speak Chinese?', can't say I'm British without 'Why didn't you learn Chinese?', can't say I'm Mauritian without 'Oh, what part of Malaysia are you from?' Listen, if I want to be English, I'll be English, If I want to be Mauritian, I'll be Mauritian, and If I want to be Chinese, I'll be bloody Chinese. I've put up with enough crap in enough countries to be anything I want. 'Cause you know what? I've earned it!

Silence.

Excuse me, jet-lag. And just... adjusting to the change... I suppose.

Let's... start again, shall we?

Good Morning. I'm Miss Chong, your new English teacher, but you can call me Alice. I love noodles and dim sum and travelling and have always wanted to come here to learn Chinese.

Get the Fuck Out
by Connor Allen

Bailey   Look, I'm going to say this to you once And once
only okay

So listen up closely
Which I know is super hard for you To actually listen
To anyone BUT yourself
But try your best yeah

Get the fuck out.

Woah Woah Woah, No

No buts and uh uh uh uh uhs

Trying to explain...
Trying to worm your way in...

Get. The. Fuck. Out. Simple as that

You don't get to rock up here after all these years.
After everything you've done.
Everything you put us through.
Regardless of the situation we're in today

and expect everything to just be okay

Pay some false respects and all that Nah fuck that

Uh, Excuse me I haven't finished. Don't like it then
fuck off

All your broken promises
The missed parents evenings leaving Mum there on

her own
all the birthdays and Christmases you weren't there
and Mum was trying to make everything perfect because she knew the only present I actually wanted,
the only thing that would make me happy, she
couldn't give me.
That present was you.
All I wanted was a dad.

To play basketball with me
To walk me to school
To talk too about my first proper girlfriend To show
me how to be a man
To just want me.
Like actually want me.

But that wasn't you.
I doubt you're even capable of that level of love.

I still haven't finished!
I don't want to hear your bullshit or your excuses It
ain't working anymore

You don't get to swagger up here and pay respects
to a woman you abandoned. You gave up that
privilege when you left.
Period.
See, if you actually cared you would've been there

Not left your 15-year-old son to care for his dying
mother Not made excuse after excuse after excuse
Constantly letting us down

Letting me down

She never let me down
She took blow after blow and never walked away
She's twice the man you'll ever be

The only promise she ever broke in 15 years was
that she was gunna stay to see the man I grow up to
be
And I promise you here today, that man I grow up
to be won't be anything like you.

But outta respect to the queen that died in my
arms, the woman that raised me and the relationship you guys once had
You can wait outside until the service is over and
come and pay your respects once everyone has left.

That's all you get
So like it or lump it
Because I gotta go in there and not only say good-
bye to my mum but to my dad too. Because even
after all the shit, I did grow up with both parents.
She was just called Mum.

Get Up, Fix Up.
by Ibraheem Toure

Kyron   Okay, time for real talk. Not to excuse myself or to be forgiven but to leave you with something that one day, trust me, will save you. I might sound brutal. I might irritate you, get on your nerves. But someone has to be the fucking sledgehammer that smashes you awake, drags you out of bed and rips open the curtains to the real world. And it's my brotherly duty to do whatever it takes to make you realise we must be a cut above the rest.

Today you had a chance to go and make something of your life and you decide to fuck it off like it's not important. All you had to do was get up and turn up and show that rahtid college that you are worth something! But nah… you decided to curl up, close your eyes and hide.

Kisses teeth.

We are blessed every single day to prove our worth…. and seeing you laying in that bed, sedated by stale inactivity… it fucking pains me, man.

Now, I am not here to make you into something you are not, and I am not saying you can't enjoy your life. It's not about being a slave. It's about changing your narrative, it's about being your own master.

Bro, this ting ain't no straight road… believe me…

Look at my life! The options I got were hindered because no one believed I could achieve. I got dashed to the side, Marcus. I got swiped left into a world where no kid deserves to be and I had to learn to survive. And I discovered that life is a mad, mash-up journey of our responses to random events that we stitch together and call our 'story'. You've got to be prepared to work, to fight, to struggle because trust me there are nuff people out there that will teef the things you deserve without a second thought of appreciation or compassion for you.

Dad couldn't fight, couldn't play the cards he got dealt… Dad folded. But us… US… my G, haha. We're gonna learn to play this game and we are gonna win. Life ain't gonna tuck you in and kiss you good-night. It will race past you and leave you in the dust and you will be 21 and look me in the eyes and ask me, 'Where did time go? How did I miss that?'

Every night as you go to bed you have prepare your mind so that every morning you can get up ready to prove yourself. But ready or not, you have to get up. The world don't wait.

Understand the responsibilities we carry. When you stand before our mother, the woman who will fight any battle for you, be the man you is, ready to un-leash his genius, ingenuity and sheer sweat to make her proud. Most importantly… Bro… when you look in the mirror always stand tall and always see a leader in his own life. A king. So many times you have made me proud. And no matter what fuck ups you've made, you have always made me love you. And I always will. I know your potential. I know your worth.

Now I beg you, stop being a dickhead and fix up.

Going Home
by Dannielle Sadiq

Shay   Ash, I'm leaving. There's just not enough space for us here. No, not just in this kitchen, that dining room, this house. Not just within these walls, but the ones out there too. And you – you just don't get it.

Every time you allowed your parents to make uninformed comments about my hair I'd tell myself, 'He'll talk to them later.' Every time you said, 'You're so beautiful for a black girl,' I'd think, 'he'll get it eventually' – or every time, you proved yourself to be besotted with the idea of shutting down any political views about race, I'd say, 'I'll just teach him.'

But I've come to learn that some things can't be taught. Or untaught. And people can only learn or change if they want to. And I don't want to be anyone's awareness babysitter, teaching them the ABC basics of how not to be racist.

No! You don't get to shudder at the word racist when you barely ever acknowledge actual racism. Laughing off family microaggressions, stereotypical accusations. You don't get to be cheerfully complicit to daily injustice. Congratulating yourself for not being racist while being too lazy and short-sighted to be anti-racist.

And yet somehow I've kept working at loving. But I'm tired, Ash. Physically, mentally, spiritually drained. Tired of telling you over and over how deeply I'm hurting, how I'm desperate for change, only to feel my soul dying inside as you fall over yourself to add a 'but' to the end of my every sentence. So, yeah. I'm leaving this so-called family gathering. And I'm going home. God only knows where that is, but it's not where we live and it sure as hell isn't anywhere we can be together.

I used to believe it was. Travelling together across Europe. Walking hand in hand around beautiful cities, discovering our own secret spots, making new memories, new ambitions, imagining new worlds. I almost didn't feel uneasiness crawling over my skin as we walked into stores that clearly didn't want to sell me anything, or your obliviousness when strangers shouted 'Obama' at me in the street. You didn't share the disgust that snaked itself around my neck as drunken people slurred at me to go back home. I tried to share your obliviousness. But that's not my heritage. That's not my life. And neither are you.

Good Witch Bad Witch
by Naomi Denny

Inside a grimy flat. ELLA (22) is trying to persuade her brother Elliot (23) to leave before the police arrive after an altercation.

Ella   Elliot. Please. I need you to listen to me. If we don't get out now, they're going to come in here in a couple of minutes with shouting and arrests and guns and we'll all be absolutely fucked. Is that what you want?

They won't give you a second chance. They won't ask anyone what really happened. They won't even listen to me when I tell them I had nothing to do with it.

Don't you get it?

They will not listen to you because they do not care.

It was decided long before we were born that people that look like you and me are the problem.

Can you hear me? Do you remember when we were kids? When Daniel Bridely punched you in the playground and then you fought back and it was you who ended up getting suspended? It's the SAME FUCKING thing Elliot, only this time there are guns and batons and handcuffs. It doesn't matter who started it, they will end it. And it will end with all of us in a cell. Or under police watch in A&E.

God, this is fucked.

She sits down, exhausted.

Do you – remember?

Do you remember the first time you realised you weren't white?

I do.

Seven years old. At a fancy-dress party, and we were playing witches. I was dressed in this pink dress and some white tights and Mum had done my hair in buns. She said it looked cute. Still does, to be honest. We were deciding who was the bad witch and who were the good witches. Remember when we thought they were two separate things? Absolutely fucked.

Anyway. They had these flower crowns for the good witches. I really, really wanted to wear one, but Arabella – yep that was her real name, god knows why Mum let me hang out with her – told me that I had to be the bad witch because I 'looked different' and so it would be easier as the rest of them would all match.

I was wearing basically the same thing as her. So I told her she was mean and then I got told off for making her cry.

This shit is ingrained and we will have to keep fighting and we will keep fighting. But we can't fight when we're locked up.

So please. Let's go.

Because this is a fucking shit place to spend your last minutes of freedom.

Carpet's got stains on it.

Guardian
by Aaron Douglas

Elijah   You've got the wrong house.

Wait! You've broken the door?! What the fuck are you doing? You're treading glass everywhere.

Harriet, it's okay, it's okay. Shhh. They're gonna leave. She's scared. Officers, you're scaring her.

Let me turn the blender off. It's just a smoothie. I'm not gonna attack you with a strawberry and banana smoothie, for fucksake. The noise; you're scaring her.

You can't just come barging in here. You've fucked the carpet up too! Your shoes! If you wanna chat with me you can point the gun away from my face. That would be great. Are you allowed guns here?! A taser isn't any better.

Hey, my hands are up, they're up! They're up. She's a baby. Let me go to her.

She's not mine. This isn't my home. But I have the right to be here; I'm babysitting. Seriously, ask the family: the Dillons. I'll call them. Let me reach for my phone, real quick? They'll be livid when they get back from their opera to find this mess!

Beat.

Don't take my phone. Fine, then *you* call the Dillons!
They'll tell you. I'm supposed to be here. Hey, listen! Look at the photographs... in the photo frames.
That's me and my mum! At Brighton Pier with the
people who *own* this house. My godparents,
Marcus and Rosie Dillon. I know them! They know
me! You honestly think I broke in or something?
What have I done wrong? You think I hung photos
of myself with my victims on the wall?!

What's your number, your... erm... you know, your
badge or police identity or whatever? You can't do
this. Let me call the Dillons! Please. You're scaring
her. Don't touch her! No, *you* better not take another step forward! No, fuck *you*!

Sorry. I shouldn't have... I've just come back from
uni, making some extra cash for family friends. I can
show you my NUS card! Or my ID or something? I'll
prove it! I'm just going to get my wallet. Slowly. Can
I just show you my wallet? Alright. It's on the side,
next to the sofa; the wallet, of course – I'm not
getting a weapon!

I've done nothing wrong. I've done nothing wrong!
What are you arresting me for? You're supposed to
read me my rights?! You are! I study law for fucksake!

Beat.

Hey, listen to me. You need to let me go. I haven't

done anything. Let. Me. Go. Why aren't you listening? Look at my ID! Alright, shit! I'm complying. I'm
down.

Beat.

Please. I'm on the ground. Okay. Just don't kill me.
Please.

Honest Funeral
by Charlie S. Smith

MARY holds some flowers, sitting by a tombstone.

Mary   Well, little bro. Mum did it. Finally said it out loud. Did you hear her?

She was rearranging the flowers on your coffin. And she said,

'I don't think I love them – the others, your siblings. At least not the way they want me to. And I've told them before, I can't give them more than what I am. I feel stuck, 'cause I can't really say take it or leave it, now, can I? They're all I've got left now that you're... I really did want them. I had waited for so long and when we finally got confirmation we could adopt, it was... a miracle!

I can't say it wasn't difficult sometimes, but we made it work.

Still, I'm not sure we were ever 'right'. At least not like you and I.

I know she wants things to be better now, your eldest sister. I can see she's trying so hard to build the connection we never had.

But if I'm okay with the way things are between us, why can't she be? Why is nothing ever good enough? With you it's different. You're different.

You're simpler. Easier to love. She always wants so much!

Too much.

Maybe it just looks like I give less to them both because they ask so much more of me. One too quiet, the other way too... everything.

And let's be honest. I carried you inside me for nine months, we can't ignore that bond. I might sound like a monster, but it's true. It's like looking into a mirror, you've got my chin, my eyes... You know it's not about skin colour, it really isn't. I can't help but see myself in you. I don't connect with the other two. And maybe I don't think I should.

It's not easy being a mum to you three, you know.

I don't know, I mean I just make it up as I go, like everyone else.

All I can say is I tried my best. But they're not you.'

Beat.

I don't think she knew I could hear her.

Hope not. That would make her a really terrible person! And she's not, trust me. She's just... You know... human, I guess is the word? Human.

I Didn't Mean to Follow You
by Nicole Abraham

Yael I didn't mean to follow you, it just happened. You know when things just happen? When things feel so right that you just can't stop, because then that would feel wrong... I just happened to get off at the same stop as you, that's all. It's not like I had to pretend I was a spy on a top-secret mission and hide around the corner each time you change direction. Because if you turned around and saw me, well... you wouldn't see me, nobody does. I just happened to take the same route as you until I reached your street and now I just happen to be sitting in your wardrobe.

Yeah, that's pretty fucked up...

But you know I said about things feeling right? Well, watching you open the door to your house just, *felt right*. And then when your neighbour called you, walking through your front door just, *felt right* – like you were opening the door for me first, before you walked in, a real gentlemen. And then after I'd had a good look around I heard you come in, and going downstairs and introducing myself didn't feel like the right thing to do, so I hid in your wardrobe. That felt like the right thing to do.

I've been sitting here for about thirteen hours now. I haven't slept, I've just been listening to you. You were humming the Harry Potter theme tune before you got into bed. And then you spoke to your mum on the phone for about 32 minutes. And *you* called *her*! And then you put *Friends* on and fell asleep three episodes later. I guess I've had many opportunities to leave now, as you've been asleep for 23 episodes, but sitting here with you just feels, *right.* It's a happy, peaceful feeling and I don't get this feeling a lot, or never. I feel connected with you and Phoebe is singing that song about the papier-mâché man and everything feels, *really right*.

From the crack in your wardrobe, I can see the sunlight creeping in. You'll wake up and so I know things will stop feeling right soon. I should leave now. I'm so pathetic. I'm disgusting, repulsive. I'm like a parasite you don't know exists – one of those repugnant, revolting tapeworms that can live and grow up to 25 metres inside you. A sick, twisted, scrounging, scum of the earth, fucked in the head leech. *(Pause.)* But sitting here still feels peaceful, and hearing the sound of your breath combined with Phoebe trying to teach Joey how to say je-ma-pell soothes me. So, I think I'll stay here, just a little bit longer.

I Never Asked You to Love Me
by Stephanie Stevens

Grace I'm not an 'emotions' person, I'm not an emotional
person. I am not emotional.

I like numbers and vertical lines and graphs and dec-
imal points and the sound of chalk on a blackboard.
I like real, tangible things that lead to something
useful. Love is not useful.

It's…

Love.

Is.

Vicious.

Love is vicious. Painful. Mysterious. Elusive. De-
manding. Excruciating. All these books and songs
and films make 'Love'. LOVE. They make it sound so
beautiful. So powerful. Like you must have it you
must feel it you must share it and if you don't your
life is empty and meaningless and dull. That is not
my experience. Love. Love starts wars. It is blinding.
It is cataclysmic. It withers. It is finite. It is flawed.

Dad said he loved my mum. Then he would beat her
until there was blood on the kitchen walls.

Mum said she loved me then she left me. Alone
with him. Dad said he loved me then he wouldn't
feed me for weeks.

When you tell me that you love me – 'I love you Grace' – you are asking me to forget what people can do. What people who are supposed to protect you, can do. And that's cruel.

I never asked you to love me. I don't need you to love me. Don't ask me to love you.

Please.

I'm Not the Disease
by Eric Mok

SAM – can be any played be anyone of East Asian descent.

Sam   You know what? I'm done. No, fuck that, *we're* done. I don't want to be around someone who doesn't think for themselves. Don't you even see how fucking toxic this is?

This isn't just a little bit of banter, Alex; laugh it off, blame it on the wine. This is my life. Every day I walk down the street and people cover their mouths when they walk past me. I get comments from strangers like, 'Go back to China and take the disease with you.' Last week I was walking home and there were two schoolgirls, I hear them whisper, 'Watch out, they might have coronavirus.' Not more than twelve years old. Fucking kids! And now, yet again, you just sit there watching your parents take the piss out of me? I don't give a shit how 'old school' they are, there's no fucking excuse. And even if we do expect it from their generation, what about you? Fucking laughing with them. What's that? Who are you?

I'm so fucking paranoid, all the time. Even when I go to the shops, I can feel people staring at me, judging me because of something that started halfway across the world. I am being blamed for something that was not my fault. I'm a scapegoat, can't you fucking see that? It's hard enough in this country being East Asian, we don't have an identity here, we don't exist. You've never had to feel like an outsider in your own country. We're invisible. I feel like a ghost, but I'm the one being haunted. We're seen as nothing more than takeaway owners and foreign students. But we have been here for so much longer than you think, and we are so much more than you think. I'm as British as you or any other person living here. I've never even been to China!

I did actually love you. I even believed you loved me. We made each other laugh, it felt good to be around you. But now... You cripple me. I tell myself I shouldn't let this stuff get to me – 'A joke's a joke', 'Sticks and stones' – but under the skin, behind the laughing it off, it does get to me, and I hate that it does and still I stay with you. And now it's years and years of the same bullshit. And I don't want to play this game anymore.

My feelings exist, whether you choose to notice them or not. I exist, whether you choose to see what other people are trying to do me or not. I'm a human being. Not a punchline. And I'm not the disease. You are.

I'm Not White

by Dee-Dee Samuels

RACHNA – White-passing Irish-Pakistani.

Rachna   I know I'm late.

I've been at the bar staring at you, trying to pluck up the nerve to walk over here and say hello.

I know I'm not what you expected.

When I told you I was mixed race I know you didn't anticipate this whiter shade of pale.

The real me was a shock to me too. Yelling at me dad during a white fiery pre-teen rage, 'I'm not a Paki – you are. I'm white!' His fiery feeling breaking like wounded weather in all directions across his face. Walking round and around me in circles. 'If I'm a bloody Paki, then you're a bloody little Paki too,' over and over like we were in some underground political spoken word off-Broadway play. The pain in his shoulders. The shame of awakening to who I was and how I'd betrayed us both.

You're shorter than I thought. Not my usual type. Lovely. You're lovely. Never thought I would agree to a blind date. But four emails later I still can't get you off me mind, Tashmin. So I'm here. Wild-haired and willing and wondering how to say hello.

Hello Tash. I want to kiss you, Tash. I want to make you forget how to breathe. The way your emails make me forget. The way I know your kiss will.

But first I have tell you everything, let you know everything about me, so that when I get lost – and I will – I can ask for directions back.

This evenin', while I was getting ready for my date with you – the perfect man made of perfect words strung together in perfect phrases – I had my thousandth impromptu identity crisis. That's why my hair looks like this. I'm there in front of the mirror and WHOOSH! I leave me body, floating up to the ceiling fan and I'm watching meself and my lifetime struggle to straighten me hair and all of a suddenness I hear me dad shouting to me mam like he did when I was a wee wild thing, 'Tie that child's hair back, she looks unkempt and unkept' – as me lily-white mam wrestles the bush of thorns on my head into a tight black braid at the back. Smooth and Caucasian at the front. There's me hovering on the ceiling, watching the very moment I was taught to erase any outward evidence of the feral girly inside. The moment I was sent down for a life sentence of hard labour.

But no more chain gang. Not anymore. Not since your words, Tash. I'm not going to live in a identity that knits my body into a prickly sweater I need to wriggle free from. Betrayed by the random white-ness of skin that makes the bartender feel safe saying the shit he just said to me about you. I don't want to be in their tribe. I want to be in yours. Ours. Be the woman you see me as. Feel me as. Help me to feel I am.

I don't get off easier 'cause I can pass for Spanish or something less unacceptable. I'm fed up with lying to the world and the world lying back to me.

I do realise this may be a wee bit much for a first date. I am a bit much. So, I'm going to excuse me-self to the loo, to comb out me hair a little wilder, and if I come back and you're still here, well then, that'll be grand. And thank you for bringing me this far.

Rachna turns her back to the audience. Fluffs up her hair. Smells her armpits. Takes a deep breath. Turns, looks around, then sits back down.

Right. Just me then. Well, it's a good bloody time to figure out who the fuck that is. Hey, Racist Waiter! Can I get a menu please?

No... Just the one.

Jew-ish
by Mical Nelken

Hila   Zeide, grandpa, I don't need you to say I'm Jewish. I
know that halakhically I am not. That's what I'm
trying to say – I know the rules, your rules. The
rabbi made it very clear. You made it very clear, all
my life, there was a blood pact, and Dad broke it.
Dad married a shiksa – so I'm out. But... When the
Hannahs and Harriets ask me, 'Hila? Interesting
name! Where's it from?' I have to tell them, 'It's a
Jewish name, but I'm not Jewish.' It took me so long
to understand and accept. I thought – if only I was
nicer, or smarter, or just better, you wouldn't be
ashamed to claim me as one of your own. I tried so
hard. I do shabbat on Friday nights, fast on Yom
Kippur, organise the family seder. I was eight years
old the first time I was called a dirty Jew; then,
when I was twelve, my classmates wrote 'dirty Jew'
in Tippex all over my books. And yet still I'm not
Jewish! Here I am. Both the only Jew child in the
village and the Shabbat goy. But there's no air here
in the middle, and I'm suffocating. Can't you, can't
you all just make some space for the grey area? For
the grey grandchild? For me?

Keys
By Jonathan Luwagga

Kato   *(Softly spoken.)* Hey babe.

Aoow you're reading my book. I LOVE *To Kill a Mockingbird*.

 Do you know what that book taught me? It taught me that despite Atticus's capable and impassioned defence of Tom Robinson, the jury still finds him guilty. And that verdict teaches Scout and Jem to confront the fact that the morals Atticus (their father) has taught them cannot always be reconciled with the reality of the world and the evils of human nature.

Right *(standing)* I need to go out, so can I please have the key? I can't find mine, and we're locked in.

Oh, where have you put my vodka? I wanna take it round Isaac's as a peace offering. After that argument.

Laughs.

What was it even about again?

Helllooo!!! I am talking to you. Vicky, you're not funny.

Don't wind me up, you know. I'm not in the mood.

Oi! Where have you put my keys and my vodka? Look at me when I am talking to you.

Okay, don't know what you think this is. I suggest you give them back to me ASAP before I stop seeing the funny side.

VICKY!!! TELL ME NOW where you have put my FUCKING VODKA and KEYS. I'm not going to ask you again. I need them right now, 'cause I'm fucking LATE and I don't have TIME for your fucking stupid games.

Okay I'm gonna count to three...

One. Two. You're asking for this...

Three.

You fucking bitch.

If it weren't for you, I wouldn't be drinking in the first place. (*Pause.*) All those fucking years of your rubbish and bullshit and stress. You were supposed to be the love of my fucking life. You were supposed to protect me. You took advantage of me and hurt me. And now you're literally hiding my fucking medication. You're a selfish piece of shit. Give me my drink and the keys, give me my FUCKing drink and keys...

Panics and hyperventilates for a few seconds, then laughs hysterically and sits back on sofa, slumped.

Fuck sakes man, I am a grown person, I have already told you, I don't need or have the time for you to play mummy.

But you know what, I forgive you for being a selfish cruel bitch, because I love you, but if you do not give me my drink back, I will smash up this whole house.

I don't even know why you're acting like I am the only person who drinks. Everyone drinks. You drink! You're a hypocrite, stop this brutal bullshit, I need MY DRINK. I need to FUCKING UNWIND and YOU'RE winding me UP!

Before I met you I literally never drank at all, except that one other time or two. And yet you have the audacity to judge and control me when you're the one who's out of control. Emasculating your man, taking away my freedom. Big mistake, darlin'. Big mistake.

Do you know what it feels like being a black man in this world? Unprovoked police stops and 'routine searches'; People laughing at you, staring at you; walking round shops with the security guard following you because you happen to have your hood up. Growing up with kids making comments about your lips, your dick-size, your motherfucking head shape?

So yes, maybe I do have a little bit of a problem, which is why I don't want to 'drink' drink, just snatch a quick sip to calm me down. Help me think. Make me feel normal for just five fucking minutes. Don't you want me to feel normal? Have you forgotten you love me? Oh. Okay. Sorry. I just thought you'd forgotten. You know your memory's been weak since you've been sober.

I promise, first thing in the morning I will go to the doctor's and get all the help I need. I just need this one drink. This one time and that's it. Once you give me my drink, we can sit down and watch whatever you want to watch, and we can talk about our ambitions like we used to, Vicky.

On his knees.

Please, Vicky, please, babe, PLEASE PLEASE PLEASE

I'm begging you. I'm dying here. I'm lost.

Please help me.

Lazy Activist
by Sabrena Osei Tutu

Genesis   It's unfortunate, I don't really have anything to tell you. I did try to think of something to say, and I wanted it to be epic, like some speech by Lorraine Hansberry – you know, the type of speech that would ignite a movement like this one; the way Alicia Garza did, or Huey P Newton, but I got nothing. I've got nothing to say. I've exhausted my last shred of sense of moral justice on fighting for my peace of mind, defending my civil right to sit and do nothing.

I bet you thought that I'd have some horrifying reminiscences to share across social media about my battle against racism, but instead of posting tributes online in support of Black Lives Matter, I've been posting tributes over chat roulette, contributing instead to a stranger's wet dream, and instead of traveling 0.2 miles within my own zone to protest, I travelled from Zone 2 to Zone 4 to sleep with a man who has never shown solidarity with black women except for solidarity with the use of my body past midnight under cum-stained sheets. That was my essential journey.

Oh, don't look at me like that, Larry. I know it's fucked, but I've been trained so well and, come on, we both know one does not simply grow out of indoctrination. My mind has been colonised, it's a pattern, you have to unlearn that shit. I'm an ill mutation of the rape and subjugation of black women: I am a living depiction of that history. I don't need to be hoaxed into submission or pulled by a metal chain leash. I go to my captors willingly now, exploiting my body for fast gratification because I only feel like I matter just before his orgasm. I do as I have been conditioned to, Larry: despise myself and expect the barest minimum.

And at a time like this, Larry, I guess you'd suspect that someone of my shade would have some armour collecting dust in the closet that I've been eager to wear for a moment like this – that's probably why you asked me to join you on that march – but honestly, Larry, I really didn't expect anything like this to ever happen, and now it's simply too late. I've already surrendered my weaponry to the oppressor.

I'm not surprised you asked, though. My skin isn't a pale enough canvas to highlight the damage that had been done in the previous fight; you can't see the scar from when I maimed myself so that my own blood could keep me warm when all hearts towards me were cold. You can't spot the stitches I got from bearing the pain from the persecution of my brother and enslavement of my father on my back whilst my limbs were being torn from underneath me. Because a black woman must live up to the expectation of her kin and has been deified as mother nature, giving selflessly of herself to all her children while they pollute her and suck her dry. Because a black woman suffers silently, ashamed of tending to her own wounds, for fear that someone will notice her sorrow and call her out for not fulfilling the perpetuated image of strong and independent, or dismiss her as crazy because her passion is too 'aggressive'.

I'm exhausted, Larry.
And now the lungs that have been ripped out of me are finally being returned, my breath is foul because my spirit is unclean. And now that my broken limbs have been casually tossed back to me, don't expect them to aid this revolt. What use are they anyway while attached to a debauched soul?

This soldier is just too fucked to attend the uprising.

So no, Larry, I will not be joining you and the rest of your Anglo-Saxon chums on your pilgrimage to redemption. I'm tapping out of the frontlines, and though I support your cause, I will be doing so by rewiring my mentality towards my reflection in the mirror and learning how to love myself, to take care of myself. This black woman. I'm going to start, Larry, by binge-watching my favourite anime and having a wank to that Nikki Giovanni interview with James Baldwin, because his intellect turns me on and Ms Giovanni's smile... is killer.

Locs

by Sèverine Howell-Meri

JULES – early 20s, any gender, mixed race, fiery spirit, warm heart.

Jules speaks as though he/she/they currently has locs in his/her/their hair. However, please alter the tenses as much as you like if you do not have locs in for an upcoming audition. Feel free to adapt this speech to braids, twists or any other style you have too.

Jules   Please stop pretending, I can see it. You are so uncomfortable around me. It's like you wanna run away as soon as I mention racism or women's rights. Avoiding all confrontation, thinking I'm 'anti men' and 'anti white', so yeah, I'm not surprised you don't like my locs.

Are they scary? Too 'next level'? Mum, we're Caribbean. They are quite literally a part of our culture. Is it because it's something that I didn't learn from you? Is that what you mean when you say they're 'not me'? It was fine when I wanted to straighten my hair for the first time; hell, you encouraged me, even. So why is this any different?

You think I was happier in school, where they made fun of my hair and my skin? Telling me I looked like a poodle, calling me a coconut and asking me which side I would choose in a war. You told me then that

I needed to stay away from those racist girls even though I wanted to be liked by them. You asked me why I didn't have any black friends and you told me I should be so proud of the black and the white in me. But now, because I've decided to wear locs and because I hang around with more black people, you're telling me you don't recognise me?

Mum, the difference between me at fifteen and me now is that I read. I'm not afraid to be curious. I could never be curious with my white friends, they all thought a Colombo curry was a tikka masala and were confused when I told them they're two different things.

Look, maybe it's different for you because you grew up there. You had your tribe, you know? I didn't find my tribe till a bit later. I can't speak creole, you can. So this makes me feel like I actually am from there too. These locs are my creole.

Beat.

I know you think they're dirty. And you think they're ugly. But I think that's because someone taught you that they're ugly.

I'm learning how to do these myself. I even did the last few back here. I know! That makes me really happy. Yeah, you say that you support that but... I think you're scared of me, Mum, and I really wish you weren't. I wanted to ask … could you help me?

I'd really love if you could help me loc my hair. Like you used to twist it when I was little by the TV. I hate it when other people want to touch my hair but I'd love it if you could, Mum. I'd love for them to bring us closer again.

Love is Gay
by Dior Clarke

Danny   Remember the day I got left at nursery on my own.

Dad walked me in, sat with me to play.

Failed to tell me he weren't intending to stay.

Turned my back to fetch some colouring pencils and he melted away. Erased

I cried, I cried, wiped my tears and continued to play. Unfazed. That the day I learned that other meaning of play.

Perform. Everything normal. Everything calm. While inside me rages a storm.

There I stood navigating and faking my way through boy to manhood.

Surrounded by broken boy role models like me.

But at least they weren't Batty Boys.

They were real Boys, real Men like we're all supposed to be.

So what was I? I mean, really? Well, I wanted to be me.

But look at me.

Dancing in the mirror, how can I be?

Fuck that shit I ain't no Batty man!

See me here I'm a real Man. Strong man. Road man. Bad Man

Definitely no chi-chi man!

Destined for fame, gotta learn to play the game.

But it keeps happening. Veneer keeps cracking. Ever since the first time him and me kissed and experimented with dry humping. This G been sweating to outrun it. Bury it. Bun it. But the secret me keeps coming. And coming. And...

Age ten – that's when I knew I was attracted to men. The touch the presence, the scent of them.

No, No, No that's wrong, unholy, disgusting,

But lying awake touching myself at night

The memory of him feels so fucking right, dick in hand, thrusting.

No!

Wipe those eyes.

No more cries. More lies.

Pray! It will go away. One Day. Continue to play. Perform Normal with precision. And my life's a Borstal. My swagger's a prison

Years going by.

Still playing that guy

Still smashing the right lies.

Ladies' boy.

Sweet boy.

All up in that pussy.

No sissy no wussy.

Bad boy.

Black boy.

Definitely no Batty Boy, I ain't, I fucking ain't.

Watch gay porn, but I ain't

Have sex with boys, but I ain't

They're straight, so they ain't

They're proper bad boys, so they ain't

and I ain't

and we ain't?

Have a girlfriend, lick pussy. Not balls and taint.

SO I AIN'T!

Peers love me, I'm a popular guy, Enemies fear me, got clout and rep.

I'm the man

Honour family show my God respect.

Bury the disease. Walk tall with ease. What next?

Marry a woman? Have kids?

Fuck these tears, continue to play and the love will persist.

Mess up and the love will go away.

So I play my part. And I stay.

And I pray.

Maybe one day. True love. Or something.

One day.

Fuck that.

Love is gay.

And a man.

Ain't

Gay.

Lucky

by Adil Hassan

Yusuf   I'm lucky? Lucky Yusuf. What the hell does that even mean, luck? Is it a fucking leprechaun that falls out of the sky and kicks you in the balls and says, 'Here's some luck, ya fucker!'?

Well, I think luck is what other people call results: when someone else has worked their arse off and... they haven't. Cos that's what I did, believe it or not. You didn't see me putting in the work, but I definitely did – and do – while you go out and get shitfaced down the pub. Now finally you know why I'm never at that type of shit. I can't afford to waste my time on bullshit; no offence.

Reality is, I've gotta work harder than you lot. Why? Just because. Because of my background, because of my skin, because of the way I look. And you know what? I don't complain about my disadvantage, cos let's face it, who cares? Not you. You don't even notice. You think I'm lucky. So I make myself lucky. I put in the work and I get my reward. Did you even apply for it? Did you research? Follow up? Did you do what was required to even be in the game? Or does that just come naturally to you, as a given? And the biggest joke is, you think I'm here because of the sensitivity of 2021, being politically correct. 'They're doing it to tick that box, throw in a splash

of colour and ooh! Now we've done our bit, everyone can now shut up! No special privileges for poor
ol' Harry and Becky, they're white, they don't fit the
quota – they have to work!'

You have no idea what it means to work.

All you see is the success, you don't want to see the
struggle. You wouldn't dare to see it.

You want to see it all as luck.

And refuse to see your own.

Mama, I'm half-caste
by Ashling O'Shea

Italics indicate the voice of a different character – young daughter; various people throughout NIRMALA's life; her mum.

Nirmala   *Mama, I'm half-caste!*

I'm coloured!

I'm not black, I'm not white, I'm colourful!

She swings her little arms as she looks up at me, beaming from ear to ear. I stare at the gap between her two front teeth as the words spill through them. *I'm not black, I'm not white, I'm colourful!*

I freeze. The words just sit there. My mouth starts salivating.

And I wonder, Mum, did you feel this sick when I came home calling myself a Paki?

I try and see the words the way she sees herself in the world.

I'm colourful. I'm beautiful and interesting and I'm not just one thing. I'm smart and funny and kind and you can't put me into a box because I'm too big to fit into any of them. I'm an astronaut and a librarian and a pirate and a vet and an artist and, and, and I'm Captain Marvel! I'm invincible.

I try to see the words through her eyes but I can only hear them through my ears.

Who's that skinny coloured girl?
She could be pretty if she was a bit lighter.
You're supposed to go out for an Indian, not bring one home.
When did you start hanging out with a Paki?

Why didn't you teach me how to handle this? I'm not trying to sound ungrateful, I know I'm lucky to have you, I know I'm lucky to have had someone provide me with all you have, but... fuck.
Where are the tools I needed you to give me to deal with this? I'm standing in front of my baby girl as she calls herself coloured and half-caste, desperately racking my brain for some memory of what kind of stuff you would have told me and –
And I'm coming up empty. We never did have these conversations, did we? Not really. You couldn't give me the tools to deal with this stuff, because you refused to ever acknowledge this stuff.

I don't know. Ignore them. Don't worry about that.
If you spent as much time studying as you do asking me questions –

I'm trying to think of all the things I wish you told me back then. Every kid has something they resent their parents for, I know, but this... This is huge,

Mum. I have to tell my baby all the words I needed to hear, with no experience of how to do it. I have to tell her about the names she's going to be called, the people who won't like her, the way she'll be looked at and treated by the institutions meant to help her, the way she'll never quite belong any- where because she's in some race limbo, the fact that, at some point, she's going to wish more than anything that she was white.

And one day she'll be angry with herself for feeling that. And angry with me.

Unless I tell her.

I have to tell her that this world is going to do every- thing in its power to chew her up and spit her out and I need to prepare her for that. The way I need- ed you to prepare me. And then I look at her gappy little smile and —

I'm not ready.

I'm not ready for her to know all of this.

Not yet. I can't do it. Mum, is this how you —

I guess I've got time, right?

Mask
by Aaliyah Mckay

Mary   Today I'm taking off my mask. I haven't told anyone yet. But I figured if I just show up to work without it, maybe no one will notice.

You see, I normally do this really cute hairstyle where I basically straighten my hair, gel it back, and then add a long... straight... tighhhhhhht pony-tail, that gives me headaches, but adds inches. And listen, the pain is worth it, because your girl starts feeling like a 12 out of 10, like a model, a stallion – better yet, like Rapunzel's ghetto alter ego, Shapunzel.

Laughs.

Today's different though. I didn't have enough hair gel, and I tried everything, shaking the bottle, squeezing it, I even cut open the bottom just to get those last bits, you know, but it just wasn't enough, so the decision was made. Mask off.

And to be honest, I'm late – so everyone should just be working and minding their business, so I can just slide in.

3, 2, 1.

Mary slowly raises her head and begins to look around, smiling awkwardly at the audience.

Hi Tim, thanks glad you like it, no Jean I didn't cut it this is my natural hair, no it doesn't take long to do, I maintain it the same way you would Pam, yup I can straighten it if I want to but I chose the afro today, yes I do know the company code of conduct Paul, what would give you the impression I'm not following it? Well, I'm wearing the same outfit I wear every week so what could possibly make you think I'm not following the company code of conduct today, oh really

Well, I come here to work, not to navigate through a sea of responses about the hair that grows out of my head, that I can't change, and that isn't hurting anyone.

Like an echo my responses are becoming distant, but always repetitive. 'No, you cannot touch my hair', 'Yes, I do have to wash it' and 'Well If I paid for it, yes, that wig I wore last week is my hair.'

It's funny how something as small as hair can divide an office. I'm here for the first time looking like myself, but feeling so disconnected from my body it's as though I'm not even present. Like I'm watching myself fight to be heard from afar, asking myself

Have I made a mistake, was this the right decision, do I suppress my reality for other people's comfortability? Maybe I should put the mask back on.

Wait! Is it me? Why am I less confident in my

natural state? Maybe me and Rapunzel have more in common than I thought – both beautiful, locked away, dreaming of being free in worlds where metaphors and similes are used to cover up the harsh realities that people will happily project their fears onto you because they'd never have the confidence to come to work as themselves.

I'm no stranger to holding other people's burdens, but this time I'll bite. Day one of me being me starts now.

Mother Country
by Timotei Cobeanu

Romain   What should I stay for, Anton? For the whole of
Europe to treat me like a disease? What should I
stay for, brother? For illegal employment as a
cleaner, or to slave in a car wash?
We're just two days and a night into a new country
and it already feels like a pack of wolves are howling
inside me. My feet are bleeding and it's getting way
too cold to sleep on the steps of misty train stations
or in empty parks.
I need to go home.

Life is not a movie, Anton. Wake up. I know that it
was Mum's last wish for us to leave and seek a
better dream, but all we have found is a sick
nightmare. Do you see how they stare at us? At how
we eat? The contempt when they hear us speak?
Yes, our homeland is falling apart. I know our people
hate the things that make you you. I feel the
injustice, too. I just wish you could find the courage
to stand up for yourself. For your truths. Because
your truths do matter, Anton. You could be the
change we've needed for centuries. If only you
would just come back. I'm sorry it's so hard for you
to find a boy at home. I'm sorry that we lost our
parents and our legacy and their protection. Christ,
I'm sorry that you couldn't be yourself. But why turn
your back and chase another life, when you could

change the life you already own? What you hoping for, Anton? Go on. What you hoping for? Hm? Boy pussy and gin? Or cheap drugs and free porn? Cos you'll be mopping kitchen floors from six a.m. to ten at night. You'll be the scum of the earth, brother. You might as well forget about your weird perfect fantasy life now, before it gets too late. The reality is, there's not a place on earth right now without a breath of hate inside of it. What makes you think you'll be better off here?

You can say it, Anton. You're afraid. It's okay. Say it: 'I'm afraid'. C'mon. Don't be shy. 'I'm afraid to fight for my rights back home so I'd rather live where someone has already fought for them. Go on. YOUR SILENCE IS FUCKING WITH ME, ANTON. You're like a cunt Buddhist monk. Christ, I could break your neck when you act like this. You know what? God despises people who give in to fear. Who run away from things. Who aren't prepared to struggle for what they seek. Just like you.

What if I shot you, now? Right there in your chest. Maybe that's what you need, after all this begging and bullying and forcing me to crawl all these miles into nowhere beside you, ha?! A nasty, beige bullet to wake you up.

It wouldn't be easy. You and I, we've been close. Ever since the moment we entered this world. First you, then me, moments later. I can remember it in my blood and bones. Those lonely seconds apart. And I have followed you everywhere ever since. Even into this new hell. But now I'm ready to tear us apart, once and for all, and leave you here... alone. With this last question to ask yourself as you starve on these strange streets: if we all forsake her, whose country will our mother country be?

Nice
by Joshua Griffin

Jonah   Mmmm you're not listening! If you could just shhh
for a second – Sorry, but, please – really, just listen,
yeah?

I am not calling you a racist. I'm just pointing something out that makes me feel uncomfortable that
could be avoided. Yeah. And I can see that you
don't get it, that's the point: I'm trying to make it as
clear as I can. For both our sakes.

So... it's like with a cat: *you* might enjoy it *(petting
motion)* but you don't know if *they* do – actually no.

Nose. If I think your – no, I'm not saying your nose is
big – in fact – if I think you've got a great nose – and
you do, your nose is *(thumbs up)* – and I just start
fondling it saying, 'I love it,' or, 'I wish I had a nose
like that.' Sure, I think it's a compliment. But I've
not asked or anything, have I? And even if I did ask,
I'm still fondling your nose, aren't I – bear with me –
'Ooh, what a nose, I just love it.'

And notice the way I say 'I love it' as if it's some
new, exotic fruit I've discovered, when in fact it's
just your nose; and it's different from mine, sure,
but me saying that doesn't make you feel nice-
special, it makes you feel not-nice-different, as in
different species. Like zoo animal different.

Which is horrible for you
because it's such an easy thing for me to do
To just... with your nose, then move on, but it's not
easy for you to articulate why you don't feel. Comfortable.
Does that...?
I'm so fucking shit with metaphors. Sorry –
Does that make sense?
It's the same with my hair. It's very – unintentional-
ly, I know – very demeaning. And I really don't enjoy
having to laugh it off. In fact, laughing just makes
me feel worse, because then it feels like I can't say
anything without it being taken as a joke, and no,
it's not all the time obviously, but – no, yes it is! And
I'm not calling you a racist, you've been amazing –
you're still amazing – but this IS a race thing, you
can't tell me it's not, because I feel it and I've been
feeling it and I've only just now chosen to mention
it. For literally the first time. And if you choose to
see it as an attack, I don't know what to do, you're
just being simple –
Uh, simplistic.
No! No, no, it's not coming out right. I didn't mean
that.
Please don't... I really hate to see you... I really
didn't mean to make you... cry.
I'm trying so hard to articulate all of this but I just, I
don't know, maybe I should have – maybe I should

have just... I really don't mean it like that. Not nice.
Aggressive. Defensive. Unnecessary. Insensitive.
That's me.
And
Sorry
I'm sorry.

Not Greasy
by Grace Xie

Jenny This is so on brand for you, Lauren.

Did you think I wouldn't say anything this time? You know about what. You literally just looked over at me and said, 'Chinese is so greasy and disgusting.' Oh, you were talking about the food? Yeah, right! So what? That's my food and if you don't like it, I don't want to hear about it. I'm done!

Why are you such a hateful bitch all the time? And you wonder why I stopped being friends with you?

Because like your acne through your foundation, your racism shows. You use slurs like filler words, and pick on anyone with a darker shade of skin than you.

I've always thought that was ironic, knowing how much fake tan you use.

Do you know why you suddenly got extra orange last year at prom?

Tesco's orange food dye. Cost just over a quid. The reaction on your face? Priceless.

Oh whatever, Lauren. You deserved it. Someone had to do something to put you in your place.

You know what? Fuck you too! Your stupid fake tan

washed off, didn't it? The stuff you say doesn't.

God, it was exhausting being your friend, standing by, watching you say random racist shit to everyone in spitting distance, even me. And I was like your crutch. Your enabler. I couldn't do it anymore.

After I bailed, I hoped you'd change. But of course you just found others to encourage you to project all your insecurities onto other people. And yeah, I admit I sometimes do miss you. But not this you. The real you. The first you.

You didn't used to be like this, Lauren.

Remember back when we first got our new bikes and were racing each other to the end of our road? I do.

I remember turning around with a smile on my face – but then I saw you on the ground. You'd fallen off, and you were clutching your knee, like you were afraid it'd fall off.

We brought you inside and my mum soothed your scraped knee with some tiger balm. She'd been cooking all afternoon, and I could smell the broth wafting through the house. She fixed you up a hot, steaming bowl, showed you how to use chopsticks – all of us laughing when you kept dropping them.

The look on your face as you ate... it was the same look I had every time I came home, feeling tired, feeling… feeling everything I did as the only Chinese kid in the whole school, having to deal with a casually racist bitch for a best friend. It all faded away with my first bite. Just like your tears that day. And the pain in your knee.

Our food – Chinese food – it isn't just something to fill your stomach. It's a part of us. A way of feeling connected to who we are, and who we've always been – despite people around us trying to make us believe we're something else. Something less. It's not… greasy. Or disgusting. And it's not your junk food.

I don't want anyone else to feel the way I do when I hear that stuff… or to feel the way you did that day you fell. Humiliated. Confused, injured, scared and alone. Those feelings stick deep in us, making us angry and cruel. It's like a disease that's hard to cure. But that's why I hung around for so long. I thought… I *knew* that you're better than that.

Yeah. I'm sorry too. Sort of.

Anyway, that's… all I wanted to say.

What? Lunch tomorrow?

Yeah. I'd like that actually. See you then.

On (Her) Grounds
by Amber Sinclair-Case

AMELIE – mid 20s, Afro-Caribbean, transwoman.

Dialogue within brackets () is written as either an intention for the performer, or to be spoken. It is at the discretion of the performer to decide.

Amelie   What is it you see?

My big lips?

My coarse, black hair?

My arse?

What is it?

What's the trigger?

Or does my face just 'fit'?

Stripped

Beaten

Black and

Blue,

Touched

Spat on

Because you

See something very clearly, right?

Beat.

Come on.

Admit it.

You put chains on my wrists

That have been scraping

My veins for centuries.

126

You made bruises on top of
Decades old scars.
My skin is history,
Layers upon layers of
Property.
And for what?
Walking down the street?
Wearing a hoodie?
(I don't have a gun.
Stop shooting)
I will show respect for all people and their
beliefs,
values,
cultures
and individual needs.
(I can't breathe)
I will act with courage and
composure and
shall face all challenges
with self-control,
tolerance and
impartiality.
(Why did you shoot me?)
You said that, remember?
When you plead
Into the void of
Justice.
No peace.
(...)

I get it.
I feel like that too.
Like you're screaming
At brick walls
In the middle of a desert.
Do I scare you?
I must.
5 officers against
One wom-
Don't give me that look.
I defy any doctor in the world to prove
I am not a woman.
Your stony stare cannot
Change the fact
I have lived,
Dressed,
Acted,
Just what I am.
A woman.
(Please don't let me die.)

Beat.

You see, officers,
I have these voices
Inside.
My people.
Pride.
They speak to me.
Whilst you deprived
Them of a voice.

Of a life.
I hear them.
Every
Single
Day.
The first time I looked in the mirror
Past the blood,
I saw
Myself.

Beat.

And that first time I'll remember
Despite how long we loved
Together we broke each other
Up, down, left, right.
In our Game Boy play
We learned to fight
Like this hatred that filled
Your bones was mine.
It wasn't.
(It's not real.)
None of it is.
This divisive weapon
You've torn through my skin
Is worn, now.
You're not holding me for anything. (I need a
pump.) I haven't asked for legal counsel. (Mom, I'm
going to college) You have no grounds to hold me. (I
can't breathe.) And there is no ground that could.
(You shot me.) I am an anomaly. (I love you too) A

black, queer anomaly to your bullshit forces. (I love you too) Force makes it sound powerful. Like it means something. In reality, you saw a black silhouette and took your bait. I 'fit' the bill and you brought me in. This incident room that has sucked the life out of so many. For nothing. So I'll ask you again. What is it that you see?

On Call

by Jason Lee

Adam   Hello. Hello?
Hi Jen, it's me,
Obviously. God I hate talking to your voicemail...
I mean the voicemail not your voice; I love your
voice!
Obviously...
Just came out to feed the parking meter and
Thought I'd try and catch you.

Sorry babe, there's been a change of plan.
Lisa just asked me to stay on late
so um, our 'sexy skype night'... will have to wait.

Where do I start?
How much time do we even have?
It's bonkers here.

It's like yesterday I was some rookie handing instru-
ments in the operating theatre.
Now, the moment I clock in, everyone can't stop
calling my name.

Me and Sean were put with some other guys being
fast tracked through training.
We thought we were out of our depth, but these
guys?

I mean how hard is it to operate a damn respirator?

Rubs eyes.

Fuckkkkkkk!...
The ball-ache workload – four-day night stretch,
that's fine, could do a full week, that's what medical
school prepared us for.

It's just...
Uh! The stares! From the new patients.
Like I'm some sort of alien monster.
'Mrs Collins, I'm not your enemy! I swear!'
'Please calm down, Mr Newman, can't you see I'm
trying to help you?' 'No I am not going to your show
my passport, Mrs Johnson, I am not the virus.'

I always hear your voice:
'Smile, Adam, just do your job, don't let them
jeopardize it.'
I know, I know. I know.

This one guy, though: Harry the Dickhead.
You can just tell he has an England flag outside
the front of his house and wrestles his son in the
living room to show off how hard he is at family
gatherings, you know the type.
Already in a pretty bad state when he got here, but
still got the energy to flinch at the sight of me.

'That's where all viruses come from. Their kind,
have you seen their culture? Proper backwards!'

You're never fully prepared for something like that.

Every day he'd make it his mission to make my life
hell, wouldn't cooperate unless Liz was there.
Week after week, just giving it lip.
You could tell when he was getting better because
he got more racist...
Until eventually he realised none of 'the lads'
or his family were allowed in to visit.
We were all he had.

And then, out of nowhere, things took a turn for the
worse.
Yesterday, while everyone was outside, clapping,
he told me that if it got any worse
he doesn't want the treatment,
he doesn't want us to resuscitate him
Jen, he –
Honestly, he was just getting better, even called me
by my actual name.

What if life is one great big stupid parking meter,
Jen?
How much time do we have left?
How do we keep track?

Jen, I need to talk to someone and I need them to
listen.
I thought I didn't. But I do.
Thought I was fine. But I'm not.
I need people to start doing the damn research
because I'm sick of explaining science and my
fucking existence to dying idiots.
I need,
I need...
I need a hug. From you.
I do want this long distance thing to work.
But
I need you right now and you're not here.
Even if you could drive down to see me we'd still
have to be apart.

I'm losing everyone around me, Jen, I don't want to
lose you.
I need a hug from you so, so much, Jen, but life
won't even let me have that.

Oops
by Winnie Arhin

Clearly panicked and uncomfortable, GIFTY is speaking to her cousin Nia on loudspeaker.

Gifty   To be fair, this was my first time and nobody warned me about the... the... Oh my God, here it comes!

Shudders with orgasm.

What on earth even is that? It's like someone shoved two packs of popping candy up there! And now it won't come out. I've been on this toilet for almost 45 minutes. You know the battery hasn't run out yet.
(whispers) It's still going. I can't call Mum, I can't call 999 – or is this more for 111?
I just wanted to see what it was like up there! It felt so good out here.

Deep gasp.

I'm gonna get sent back for this! You know that was always the threat when we were younger.
Did you hear that happened to Kofi? He got excluded from school and got caught shoplifting pick 'n' mix from Poundland. Next thing you know gone, gone, gone! Auntie Claudia came back to London with his passport and NO him!

Can you imagine?

Mum will probably think I was taken over by the devil, but I just wanted to see what all the fuss was about! And now I've bloody lost it.

Well not lost, lost – I can still feel my bullet vibrating but obviously I can't reach the off button when it's um... unreachable at this time. Literally... unreachable. I tried to grab it before it went all the way up and I just hit the button and changed it to the dot dot dot setting –

Mimics sound of increased vibration.

I WhatsApped Nicole and all she did was send me a voice-note of her cracking up! Cow! And Priyah read it and didn't even reply – you know there's always that ONE friend that replies a week later – *(Raises her voice, clearly exasperated.)* THIS is what you call time sensitive! Here comes another one!

Holds back orgasm sound as her whole body tenses and shakes leaving her shocked and embarrassed.

What the hell is happening? It feels good but my legs go all funny and I get serious under-boob sweat, then I sort of feel like I'm having an asthma attack BUT a good one whenever the tingles start. OK... okay... okay, plan B, you're right it's unavoidable – I've got Mum's barbeque tongs – I'm going in!

I can do this – I can do this – I can do this! 3... 2... 1... hold on, I didn't lock the –

Snaps her head to the right and looks mortified.

MUM! ...it's not what it looks like!

Oversharing
by Isaac Ouro-Gnao

Edem   I know we haven't been dating for that long so I
don't want to scare you off with this But Basically
Every time we're together I keep noticing little girls
– I know it sounds weird
Just hear me out
Like last week when we met up for brunch and sat
next to the small water fountains that sprout from
the floor by the strip behind King's Cross and St
Pancras International?
Yeah I saw this little girl fitted in Green and Black
rollerblades dashing through the watery maze
Dodging their ambush so swiftly And I smiled You
know how you always call me out about that teethy
smile I have with no emotion in the eyes
Yeah Not that This felt real Like when you make me
smile But a bit different A full face smile like I was
witnessing the daughter you and me could have She
felt so familiar
Her dark skin dazzled under the wet watery jets as
they rose and fell to her rhythm Her Yellow T-shirt
covered in sunflowers and Red dungaree shorts
with one strap up and the other draped down was
actually so wavy I got envious And her hair Full
Black Afro hair Dancing Glowing under that high sun
I wanted to join in her freedom Run to her and
leave you watching us with those soft eyes you rest
into the corners of me Until the girl in you couldn't

sit still anymore and erupted and brought out the
boy in me and joined then led us on a quest of
mischief

And we'd laugh till our cheeks stung And our stom-
achs achieved Olympian form And you'd turn to her
with your crown and whisper into her hair all the
affirmations that were rationed from you And kiss
her skin with all the love denied you

And I'd lift her up and show her the heights stolen
from me And tell her my shoulders would be a
throne she could always return to

And we'd proclaim her royalty

And arm her with all the Morrisons And Giovannis
And Maathais And Winnies

All the Busbys And Blackmans And Copelands And
Lintons For all the white spaces she'd have to navigate For all the self-love and power she'd need to
maintain her infectious joy

My therapist says I have a problem with oversharing
Did I do it again?

Phone Call to Society
by Jada Wallace-Mitchell

AMELIE is stood inside what looks like an old phone box. Inside it is very futuristic and instead of speaking to a phone she speaks towards a camera and is being recorded. On the other end of the 'phone' is SOCIETY.

Amelie   They say if you make confident poses in the mirror you actually feel more confident. So there I was stood this morning, smiling, looking at myself. Blemish there. Check. Scar there. Check. Non-Eurocentric nose there. Yep, check. Nothing's changed overnight. Of course it hadn't. I don't think I expected it to, but I still had to... check. You know? Kind of like how when you're dreaming, you tell someone to pinch you to see if it's real, I don't know why, because some people actually do feel pain when they dream – but anyway, to be completely honest I don't think I wanted my features to change, but...

Beat. Trying to find the right words.

My thoughts, I wanted my thoughts to change. If my thoughts had changed, that would mean society would have changed. That you would have changed.

I know my worth. I know I'm pretty. I stood in that mirror smiling to myself because it was one of those days when I think, 'DAMN YOU'RE GORGEOUS.' But I put this request in years ago, so I fail to understand why it hasn't been processed. Which led me here to confront you face to face and ask – demand – that you tell me why nothing has changed.

Do you get off on it? The power. Does it make you feel good about yourself? Do you get a little tingle up your spine? A little bit of excitement? Adrenaline? Do you pat yourself on the back? 'Kept another one down'? Reinforced your superiority reign? Reinforced your colonial claim? That I should think that I am below your standards? Your never-ending ladder that seems to get longer every time I try to climb it.

Yes, I've asked you why, why you can make the world at peace for my friend Kennedy, the world eco-friendly for Dylan, but you can't do this one simple thing for me.

But what you don't know is that I have you figured out. I'm clued up and I've concluded that you're pathetic. Why did I ever believe that I needed your approval? My scars are stars, they show that I am living and breathing, making mistakes and learning. I was not given perfect skin, but I have learned to love it and that is growth, something that a 'perfect' skin person could not possibly claim. The bridge of my nose is thick. But it allows the smells of spices –

cinnamon and cumin – to explode into my senses from beautifully tasting foods. My skin is black. An infinite amount of shades and stories, unfathomably beautiful, the culture and colours simply exude from a look. *(Cynical chuckle.)* My lips are big and luscious, and you love it in the magazines and hate it on me, but these lips tell stories from generations before. Stories of great grandparents coming during the Windrush and working so hard that the rest of the family comes in on a plane. My hair is wild. It curls, shrinks and straightens but it is the crown that you cannot and will not take away from me. You may not appreciate these facts, but they are facts all the same, which I have decided to treasure, regardless of your views. I don't need society to fuel my self-esteem and that *(beat)* is the best gift you could have given me.

Picking Fruit with Tas
by Omar Bynon

Sim   Tas. I'm gonna leave London. Tonight. Just hear me
out. I deserve to feel satisfied at the end of the day,
innit. I deserve to feel like I've accomplished something, learnt something important, helped someone
– helped myself, for fuck's sake. But I don't feel
that, don't even feel like the day is finished yet – so
I don't sleep. Or if I do, it's a two-hour blink and I
wake up groggy as fuck, still full of yesterday's
stress. I never ever dream any more. Like I don't
deserve it or something. Well, fuck feeling like that.
I'm done hating myself – like there's something
wrong with me, when really it's there's something
wrong with this fucked up city.

I was thinking, Tas, how long would it take to walk
out of London? How far am I from a meadow? From
a sky where I can see the stars – not London stars:
Van Gogh stars. And I realised, there is nothing
keeping me from finding out but myself. So I tiptoed
downstairs, left a note by the kettle saying I'd be in
touch in a few days, and slipped out. And I thought I
was walking out of London but as I crossed Hackney
Marshes, I realised I wasn't, I was walking to you.
And I realised... yeah... I realised it's you. You're
what's keeping me here. You are the real London or
home or my everything so... come with me?

I know it sounds wild and I know you've got uni, but we both know you're just doing that shit so you can get a piece of paper in a couple years, and what's a piece of paper compared to a Van Gogh sky? We could just walk together – walk until we wanna rest, and then rest until we wanna walk again. No more rushing. No more twelve-hour shifts washing up, no more deadlines, no more noise. We'll have pub lunches and picnics and we'll sleep in the grass, or the forest if it's raining, or some nice villager will take us in, and we'll just forget about this too big, tiny fucking city. And all the tiny people lost in it. It will just be us and the 500 quid in my account that Eddie paid me on Friday, and when that runs out we can work on a farm for a bit, or pick fruit or some other rural shit.

I understand if you don't wanna come and this might be goodbye and if it is I'll just go. But it would be more fun with you, and your life depends on getting out of here as much as mine does

So what you saying? Am I walking? Or are we?

Picture Perfect
by Romayn Rose

Zora   Have you ever wondered how many random
pictures you've been in by accident? It's a weird
thought, right? Sometimes I wonder how many
photos are out there with me in the background,
looking confused... on my phone... walking to work,
arguing with someone. Listening to music. Maybe
just an arm or one of my sexy legs.

Every day billions of pictures get deleted because
the person who took it didn't think the lighting was
quite right or because the person in it didn't think
they were looking Insta ready. But if we could look
at all those pictures years later I wonder what story
they would tell. Would we get a better picture of
who we were? Whether we were sad more often
than we remember. Maybe laughed too much – if
that's a thing. If we were explorers, or like hamsters
running round and round the same places. Whether
we travelled more in groups or alone. A proper
David Attenborough look in a old mirror we thought
we'd smashed or thrown away.

Then I wonder, how many people trashed their
photo because I was in it? The unaware photo-
bomber jumping around in the background. Maybe
they wanted a picture of just themselves. Selfish.
Maybe they didn't like the way I looked. Judgy.

Why? What's wrong with me? My expression? It definitely wouldn't have been because of my clothes.

I guess they didn't want me to be part of their story.

Imagine a time in the future without cameras on our phones – it's a strange thought, I know. What if the power to delete lay completely with the oppressor? Perhaps changing the perspectives between the oppressor and the oppressed. The story only recorded from one angle... the other viewpoint edited, Photoshopped, deleted.

Selected to alter our perceptions of who we were... who we are... who we hope to be.

That's how it was not so long ago, really. Newspapers. TV. Magazines. History books. The powers that be deciding who gets celebrated. Elevated. Included. And who gets crucified, demonised, laughed at, fancied ...or left out.

Imagine what would have been if we'd been left to our own devices, what we could have seen and learned and cried and laughed about!

Well, now the power is in my hand. This little magic box allows me to control the narrative. It excludes them from deleting me from history. It stops liars from controlling the narrative and from denying and burying their ugly truths. They can't hide and we

can't be hidden. We need to make it his-story...
her-story... our story. We need to make it our own
version of picture perfect. We need to tell and
record.

Our stories. Our lives.

Plastered
by Tricia Wey

Olu   Okay, so I walk in the room and I'm scanning
around, looking for this guy, yeah? And immediately, I'm like T'Challa at that first Wakandan press
conference. It's like, 40 white faces looking at me
over their crystal stemware. But it's the old men
that get me. Old white men, looking me up and
down like the eagerly anticipated main course at a
dinner party that's running late. You know the
looks. Ranging from ravenous beasts wanting to
sink their teeth into my dark meat, to disappointed
blank gazes, wondering how I even found this place
because *(affected accent)* 'She doesn't belong here;
she's clearly lost.'

'No, I'm not lost,' I say. 'I'm actually here on a date.
Although the way that everyone in here is looking at
me like they've never seen a Black person in the
wild before makes it pretty clear that I most definitely should **not** be here on a date. What's so fas-
cinating? Surely you know that people who aren't
white can be in fancy places too? Or perhaps we're
only allowed on council estates and in music videos? Didn't have too much of a problem being
around us when your ancestors were robbing us of
our cultural artefacts so they could fill up your

museums for you to go and gawp over, though, did you?'

Beat.

Except I don't say that. I just think it. I'm actually a millisecond away from turning around and running right out, but then he's there, arm on my lower back, no questions asked, because **of course** he wouldn't ask for consent before touching me.

More touching as he places a presumptuous kiss on each cheek. But before I can even get angry about it, I'm just thinking about how thin his lips are...

He steers me to a booth that he definitely slipped a fifty to the server for, because this table is basically a podium, slap bang in the middle of the room. And as we're walking through, I feel like a prize pig trying to win a blue ribbon.

Or like a show pony at that Mascot race all them fancy white people wear those massive hats to.

I'm still considering leaving but, honestly, a bitch is hungry and I could never afford this place. So, I have a strict word with myself and command myself to suck it up... and order the most expensive thing on the menu...

...and the first thing out of his mouth is: 'You're beautiful for a Black girl.'

He says it so confidently, full of schmooze, eye-brows raised. Because to him, this is a compliment.

'You're cocky, even for a white man,' I... almost... say.

But she's more British than she wants to be. Knows where her bread is buttered, so it's a forced smile and a 'thanks' squeezed out through gritted teeth. Immediately followed by, 'Can I get a raspberry mojito?' Ding! Smile widened, charm ramped up to 10, because alcohol is needed.

He orders it and launches into a **very** indulgent monologue about how much he loves exotic women and how great my arse is. Every time he says the word exotic, I add another cocktail on to my mental order. If nothing else, by the end of this date, I'm gonna be fucking plastered.

Poppy
by Hosanna Johnson

Auden I'll be honest. I thought that too, I did. Thought they
aren't complex enough for like, having a sexual ori-
entation. I thought it was just hump; baby, hump;
baby, for them, and thus continues the circle of life.
But I was so wrong, you know? So wrong. I think
Poppy is gay, or a lesbian. Can you call a dog a lesbian? Should I call her queer? I'll call her lesbian. I'm
telling you, Poppy is a lesbian dog. She shouldn't
mind me outing her. I'm really proud actually, she's
advanced. Not just after sex for reproduction like
other animals but for sheer pleasure, like most of
us. I started to figure it out when I'd take her for
walks and sometimes she'd just pull at the leash for
certain dogs, or just the bitches. I didn't know why
at the time. I'd take her to the park and let her run
around. Once, she got a little too excited with the
ladies if you catch my drift. I found out she's a top.

At first I thought she was just a horny bitch, we've
all been there. She's probably almost a teenager
in dog years, so it could've been like a surge of out
of control animal hormones. But once there was
this male dog interested in her, he was keen but
not over, you know? Charming. I thought she'd
welcome his advances, with her being so hungry for
it. She flew, she was gone. I almost lost Poppy that

day and that's when I knew. I googled it and there's this whole history of queer animals, even sheep. There was this story about a gay ram that had to mate with hundreds of ewes on a farm, yeah. Any straight ram's dream, but this ram, he kept trying to mount the other rams. Do you know what farmers do to gay rams? They killed him, sold my g to Tesco because he was gay. Can you imagine if that ram was a person? Selling them, it's mad.

Bet that's what my dad would do to me. He'd probably sell Poppy if he knew about her. She is living proof that being lesbian or gay or queer is natural and I was raised to think it wasn't. Poppy has changed me in that sense, I wouldn't've told anyone before about it, being raised Christian and slightly homophobic, but yeah it's out now. I feel kinda bad for freaking out about it at first, because I really do love Poppy, you know? And it's just I didn't know know better before, but now I'm cool with it, 'cause she's cool with it. And that's cool.

Put Me Through
by Naomi Soneye-Thomas

Tola   Hi, sorry, yes could you please put me through to
Gemma? Yes, Gemma Williams, thanks.

Beat.

Listen, Gemma, I get that maybe it might have been
a mistake or something like that but erm, I've seen
some other people's pay slips and I just couldn't
really understand why mine was so low and... you
know, it's alright. I get it, these things happen but –

It's just... There's things I've had to miss out on.
Family things. Big birthdays and stuff whilst I've
been working overtime on projects and – you know
– that's why I thought I'd talk to you about it, cos
erm –

And I get it, you know, I've kinda been prepared for
this so I'm not... I'm not angry, it's just... You know
how our parents always tell us we'll have to work
twice as hard to get half as far and – well I guess
you don't, cos your parents wouldn't cos you're...
well, you're –

How could you understand? There's no way you'd
know how it feels to have all this – this pressure. I
don't feel like I ever saw my dad happy till he took
us to Nigeria. Like, of course, I'd seen him smile and
laugh and drink Guinness and all that shit but I'd

never actually realised that that wasn't him. I thought I knew him. I didn't. Until we stepped off the plane in Lagos and it was like, his aura just changed. How he carries himself there is different. Like he's qualified. Which he is.

Think about everything he gave up. For us. And you're ripping me off and I've never once spoken up. It's such bullshit. My so-called bosses. You lot in accounts. Bullshit. Treating me like a dickhead. I worked hard for that money and now you think it's cute to take the piss! Well, fuck that. I'm done. Take your fucking – sad little job and shove it right up your arse, yeah? 'Cause I am over this shit and you, Gemma, are an evil lazy fucking thief of the soul. Hello! Have you hung up on me?

I swear to God Gemma if you don't fucking say something I'm gonna come over there and lose my shit for real. Trust me, you ain't seen angry. You ain't seen rage!

What you mean, you think you might have the wrong Gemma...? Yes, um, yes! Please put me through... to the... other... Gemma.

Beat.

What the fuck? I clearly – I clearly said Gemma Williams, didn't I? These people really fucking get on my –

154

Oh hi! Hi Gemma, yeah, good to hear from you too. Yes, it's been – I've been good I – listen I erm, I mean I just wanted to say that – to say that... I've just, I've got a really bad thing. Stomach thing so, I won't be in today, is that okay? Ah amazing, thanks – yep, I'll be back in on... yeah, back on Monday.

Yeah,

Can't wait.

Questions

by Stephanie Stevens

Patrick You say you saw the video. That video.

And you have questions.

Questions?

You know there's multiple videos.
Right?

Videos.

Plural.

How many? I've lost count. So many names. And those are the people who were lucky. 'Lucky?' Who were fortunate enough to have a witness. To have someone bear witness as their life was taken. By someone with a shiny badge, a blue uniform and a powerful workers' union, who there and then decided the value of their life.

And still you have questions.

We've been friends, best friends, forever. And now you have questions. You've stayed over at my house, ate my mum's food; during P.E. in Year 8 you split your football shorts trying to do a bicycle kick and I gave you my spare shorts and I'm pretty sure you still have them; we've shared clothes. We've shared our lives. And whether or not you choose to see it, this whole time I've been Black.

And apparently you've been 'nice'.

'Nice'. What what what is 'nice'? What do you mean when you say, 'I'm nice.'

'I am a Nice person.'
'I am Nice to you.'
Is that all I can, we can, Black people can, hope for?
'Nice?'
'Pleasant.'
'Tolerant.'

Tolerant tolerance tolerate. I am something that 'nice society' tolerates. Do you know what that means? Do you know what that feels like? To be tolerated. Like some stain that can't come off?

You want to know why I don't talk about this? Why I've never brought it up to you? Why we've never talked?

I have a whole set of Black friends that you don't know about and who don't know about you. I have parts of myself that you don't know about. Does that move you? Does that make you feel anything? Does that make you understand?

You know what, I have a question. For you. Actually, I have questions, for you.

Why are you suddenly so curious? Why are you asking me? Because your world is burning down and you don't know why? Because I am your one Black friend? Feeling guilty? Feeling afraid? After all these years of switching off the TV when they talk about 'race relations in Britain' but crying your eyes out for the sad starving black babies and donating a fiver to Comic Relief? You want to save me? Rescue me?

Or do you want me to rescue you? From the shame. Eating away at you. Keeping you up at night.

When everything changes – and believe me, change is coming, who will you be? When all this is torn down and burned to the ground, who will I be to you? Who will you be to me? Who will you be to you?

Who will we be?

Sent Down
by Myles Devonté

Marcus So, we get to this huge country club in a little village outside of Oxfordshire. Abba blaring from an outhouse in the background. I'm wearing her father's old dinner jacket, this double-breasted thing, far too big for the average man, lapels out to here, apparently made me look like Eddie Murphy in *The Nutty Professor*.

Beat.

Well, they didn't know any better, you know?
And they weren't far off, all I was missing was
A moustache and about 8 stone.
But anyway, the food.

We're talking Cornish sea bass, miso glazed artichoke drizzled and dripped in smoked butter sauce.

Oh, and the starters, my word! Who knew salmon could take that many forms? Astonishing.

There I was sat drinking a bottle of bubbly in the company of the woman I loved. Talking about the places we wanted to see, the books we'd read once we got there.

In that singular moment I felt like I belonged.
Allowed to just be me.

Just be, for once.

I was never allowed to do that here. It was always made clear that my 'black' wasn't in line with their 'black'. I had to walk like them, talk like them. I stripped away me to become them. Another black boy from the estate. Nothing less, nothing more. A faceless member of the crowd, a number.

When I got accepted into Oxford I vowed to never come back here, to never wear that mask again.

Laughs to himself.

Little did I know.

Three G&Ts later I made my way to the outhouse, my normal swagger now a wobbly stride as I headed to the bar for a fourth. The music changed from Abba to rock as I drunkenly navigated my way through flailing arms and swinging jaws.

Helen's brother Archie spots me from the bar. He nudges his friends and they all burst into laughter, pointing at me, goading me with their smiles. Then he mouths the word. Nigger... and I am marooned, lost in a sea of mistaken identity. I feel my brain dissolve into my flesh and suddenly I'm on autopilot and the black boy from the estate is back. I scream as I pummel into him.

The room explodes in silence as if I've bludgeoned the DJ too. And all the pretty white faces turn black with horror. Unified in their absolute fear of me. Othello in his final moments.

I was sent down from Oxford. *(Kisses teeth.)* Nah fuck that, they kicked me out. Helen left me soon after.

Swatted from their world with ease, as if I were a fly.

Now I stand here with no place to go, wanting to start again because I'm tired of running.

I'm sorry I left you like that, Mum.

I'm home.

SHALLOW
by Karis Crimson

Nancy   And there it is! For a moment there I thought I'd
entered *The Twilight Zone* or something – that I'd
travelled to another dimension where you had
suddenly decided I wasn't the right candidate because I was just too good, but of course that was
never gonna happen, was it!

Humour me for a second though, will you, before I
go? Tell me exactly what else I'd needed to have
done to qualify for your shortlist? Hmm? Because
you've seen my resumé; you've seen what I can do,
I know you have. What about me wasn't up to par?
Because I spoke to the guy you hired when I went
for a cigarette just now, and he told me that he'd
had no prior experience, and came here because it
was 'something to do for the day'.

It's funny. The whole reason I even applied for this
job is because you told me your company was so
'forward-thinking', so 'inclusive' and 'committed to
promoting excellence and diversity at every level'.

Well, you can imagine my surprise when I walked
through the foyer this morning, passing about thirty
people and seeing not an ounce of diversity. I'm a
reasonable woman, though: I thought maybe you
just hide all the diverse people upstairs, in the
conference rooms where they are making all the

important decisions and whatnot. And then I got into the waiting room with all the other candidates and I thought to myself, did I pull up in the Mystery Machine?! Because I'm about twenty seconds away from calling Scooby and the gang to set a trap so we can catch someone! Black, Asian, Hispanic, Creole, anyone!

And even after sizing the place up, I still hung onto hope, thinking maybe this is a new initiative and you were embarrassed to tell me, but that's okay because maybe I'll be the first! Maybe I'll be the Kamala! But no.

I'm 'not what the team is looking for'. What does that even mean?!

Oh, oh I know! It wasn't enough of a sob story for you! You wanted to feel like you've made a massive difference, right? Like you're Angelina Jolie plucking a kid right from the slums of third world poverty or something. Like this opportunity was gonna change my big brown life and you'd be able to tell your friends at the yachting club how I begged and begged?

That's the thing about people like you, it's not enough to just see someone who is a different colour, you want someone who can give you the whole trauma porn experience.

Don't think I didn't notice you get irritated when I

didn't give you the responses you were craving. You're so used to the crap your racist little diversity training pamphlet tells you I should have that you can't bring yourself to dig any deeper.

Why did you even speak to me in the first place that night? Did your brown girl fetish rear its head? Did you think that if you wooed me with prospects of equality that I'd just drop my knickers for you and you'd be able to live your sick exotic fantasy or something?!

Do you know what? Forget it. I don't want to know anymore. I don't care enough. Because whatever you say is just gonna be an automated response isn't it? And you'll keep giving me automated responses until eternity because that's all you know how to do.

Lucky escape for me, I guess.

Silence
by Daniel Reid-Walters

Eden   Is a black life worth less than a white life, Andy?

It's a simple question for a simple answer: yes or no?

So, Andy Bennet-Wilson, is my life worth less than yours?

And you see, that's the problem: you're silent. Do you think by saying nothing you remain neutral, or un-opinionated? Well let me tell you, it's the complete opposite. You're actually choosing to be a bystander as black people get killed, attacked, discriminated against for something they can't change. No, I wasn't attacked physically tonight, that is truth, but words carry weight. Don't they, Andy? When I asked you out on our first date, when you asked me to move in with you, when I said yes to your proposal, those words carried weight. But let me tell you that ignorance is heavier than all that combined.

Honestly though, this isn't even about the bullshit that came spewing out of your uncle's mouth tonight. This is about you. You, who proudly holds my hand in public. You, who was so excited to first introduce me to his parents. And you, who I know would be the best dad to our kids anyone could ask for. But that's the same man who, in the face of naked prejudice, discrimination and racism, failed to stand up.

And worse than that, Andy? So did I. I'm so angry at myself, 'cause I really should have said something, but I didn't. I'm sat in a house filled with white people, and just me alone with only my fiancé for backup, and I was scared. That's the only excuse I've got, and it's not good enough. But listening as your whole family laughed really shocked me. Of course, nothing should shock me anymore about this world we live in, but some situations still take me by surprise.

And you know what, Andy, I'm tired. Tired of being ambushed in safe spaces. Tired of the need to educate people about what they should consider to be racism, and arguing for change in mindsets built up over generations, on foundations of arrogance. I'm talking about people like your uncle, spouting crap about because he's 'an Englishman living in the "least racist" country in the world', the word Nigger means less in his mouth than in an American's. He's the type of person that won't own their racism, but instead decides to wallow in it, as if bigoted opinions are something to be fucking proud of.

Can you imagine what's been said behind our backs over the five years I've been in your life? The thought alone makes me feel sick to my stomach.

Andy, this won't happen again. Not like this. You do

what you have to do, but I won't look to you for backup in this type of situation ever again, and guest or not, afraid or not... next time, I will not be silent.

Silver lining
by Amina Koroma

Amirah Salma, what is this behaviour? I can't tell if you're dense or actually have something against me, because you really moved mad on this one.

I've made it clear to you, crystal, that I have no interest in your brother whatsoever. Hakeem? Peanut head, with the sugarcane body to match – nope, absolutely not. Besides, we're cousins and I'm not about that life. Yeah, we were keke-ing at the time, but I shut it down real quick 'cause that's how people get a foot in. Family then does two plus two equals fifty, next thing you know they're married and popping out babies. Issa no from me.

Wallahi I thought that was the end of it, so tell me why I get a dm from a complete rando of my picture with the caption 'Happy birthday bae', drip, tongue emoji?
Pree this photo: my house, my end of exams party, six of us. The other girls left by the time I had this outfit on and we were in our feels with Chloe x Halle. It wasn't hard to sus out. You and your twin. Am I right, or am I right?

Nah, don't start. I'm not hearing no excuses. Fact of the matter is, you gave him access to me where you had no right to. What was private should've stayed private, *khalas.*

I block him off social media, he keeps coming back. Next thing you know, he has my number, which I've had to change and you're not getting. Me airing him must've made him feel some kinda way, because he sent voice notes and now dick pics, *wa iyyadubillah*. Side note, I was right! His head isn't the only thing that's peanut shaped. See intuition.

If the situation didn't have the potential to go left, I'd truly be laughing my ass off, but seriously, you know the script. 'Come and do something with me one time and no-one will know.' Lies, obvs. Now he's threatening to post the photo in the family group chat, accusing me of bringing men to the house, dressed like that.

Now if you, who was actually there, was brave enough to tell them the truth – which you won't – would they believe you? No. And that is what? Delusion. Family goes into crisis mode and they'll try to hook us up anyway to stop gums flapping. All because we were doing up Chloe x Halle choreo?

Let the g.c. blow up, I actually don't give a shit any-more. If this situation gives me the opportunity to up and leave this place, I'll take it. This might finally be my way out.

Sliced
by Warren Mendy

A young woman shares her experience of going through FGM.

Fatoumatou This is what they did. This is what they did, this is what they did this is what they...

Did.

I didn't die that day, but a part of me, it passed away. Part of what made me a woman was sliced, ripped, torn away from me... The lies I had been fed fell on me and fell on me hard. I want to explain to you EVERYTHING THAT HAPPENED TO ME THAT DAY.

When my grandma took me to that place, I felt excitement, as though I was becoming a real woman. And then the cutting started.

This woman – this stranger cut me so deep, as though she hated the woman in herself. I felt the core of my being shredded... I was drowning in MY OWN blood screaming in PAIN. No amount of anti-biotic, paracetemol or any medicine could have prepared me for this... nothing.

And all my grandma could say was, Well done... She was proud of me... I was a 'woman'. My anger towards my grandmother cannot consume me...

I don't want to blame her... It's all she knows; how she was raised and taught. How can I be mad at her madness? She is a product of her own pain and all that came before her.

My mother had warned me to not do it yet I still agreed, even begged and fought to have it done, therefore is it not at least a little my fault? Twelve years old. A woman.

I couldn't walk, pee or sit properly for fourteen long days. I couldn't go to school for a month and I couldn't tell anyone what happened to me. It was the shame I felt. No boys approached me: because I became so socially awkward, none dared. No one begged for me, no one brought cows for me like my grandma promised they would. No one.

My first sexual experience on my honeymoon was so painful, it took me a YEAR to even try to have sex again. The happiest day of my life was the last, as this morning I finally gave birth to my beautiful daughter. Her name chosen while still in my belly.

And now I felt myself slipping away, at every push another part of me slowly disappearing from my body, until all of me was gone. Eighteen years old and never to be a day older. With a beautiful daughter that I will never get to hold. Aissa will never have a mother to play with her, braid her hair, give her the advice I wish I had taken. She will never know me. Those who knew me will forget me, history will erase me... For what? What was the aim? The point of all of this?

I'll never know.

Stalemate

by Amina Koroma

MIRIAM, 25+ Black African / Afro-Caribbean.

Miriam   You wanna have this conversation now? Okay. Sit.

Look, Adam. The bottom line is I'm trying to revive our sex life. We were good at the beginning, then it got patchy, now it's non-existent. You think we're fine? We're not fine, because something's up with you and you won't admit it. You've been working longer, constantly tired, your diet's out of whack 'cause you barely eat when you are home. Where the fuck does Intimacy come in? Or sex? Remember sex, Adam?

So, the toys you've found are a solution. I had a whole plan to introduce these to you but, as we can see, you dislike surprises.

Yes, I used them, to see if they lived up to the reviews and the reviews did not lie. I won't lie to you, it was amazing – honestly, these are game changers – but I want you in on the fun, so join me. Try something new, spice things up a bit. Seriously though, I was cracking up when I looked these up on the 'net like, 'It does what now? How?' Opened up a whole new world, I tell you.

Demo number one: vibration ring. Lube up, slide it

to the base, get some good vibrations and up he goes. Get the ring to my clit and I get good vibes too. Win, win. And this... is a wearable for me. Hmm, how do I describe this? A clip? I dunno. What I do know though is that you insert this part, this side sits on my clit, but leaves space for you to –

Adam, really? You brought this up, and you're giving me nothing? Not even a little bit excited?

Look, don't freak out, okay?

I saw the results. You left them wide open where anyone could read them, so I did.

You knew, deep down, we both did. Your erectile dysfunction is rooted in trauma and it's okay to have trauma, babe. No one is perfect, stop trying to hold everything down.

Your body is trying to protect you, but not in the right way and we can address this. This, you, us, it can be fixed, it's curable.

I didn't say you're sick! Listen to me. We have to say it out loud because it means we acknowledge it and we can move forward. We have to talk.

You remember how it was, don't you? How we would stay in bed all weekend, those we-don't-give-a-fuck-getting-up-because-we're-fucking weekends. Just exploring each other, talking, laughing, making love? Like we're the only two people on the planet.

I miss that, I miss you. I love you, Adam, and I want to support you, but we've got to do the work, and I can't do it alone.

Truth is, I'm not satisfied with where we are and I'm running out of options. I love you and I want to make love with you, but I focused on you so much I neglected myself. I've lost touch, with me. There's no rush, but I'm gonna make the first move. I will love and make love to myself, because I deserve it and I can't wait anymore. If you refuse to choose us, I will have to choose myself.

Statement
by Tolú Fagbayi

Black Female   Hello…?

No response.

Hello, officer…?

No response.

Hello, I need to talk to an officer…

Police officer…

No response.

Now!

Pause.

Hello – My name is –

Pause.

My name is Abimbola, I, erm… I received a phone call about making a statement about my –

Pause.

About my…

Pause.

I know you think this is just another black body, another stigma but he was my boy. My eight-year-old. And I know you're not going to do anything about this – as per usual.

I'm just another black woman weeping, seeping and deeping my loss.

You know my beautiful black boy... my beautiful boy, it's only been three months since his –

His death.

I try to keep him alive in my mind, by carrying my faith with my cross in my hand. Trying to keep faith close to my heart. But... I'm turning impatient. God forgive me.

Pause.

Did you know that he isn't even mine, well of course he's mine, but... He's mine.

It's not one of those 'stories' like how white people adopt a black baby because they want to do the whole white saviour complex, my experience is different.

My partner and I were trying to conceive and I had so many miscarriages... too many to name, so my partner and I, we decided to go through the adoption process and when we saw Nathaniel's beautiful face, (his name actually means gift from God), we just knew...

We've had him for eight beautiful years – I mean *I've* had him. My partner and I aren't together anymore.

And now my boy is dead. They stabbed him in the head. I don't know who 'they' are – I don't want to know who 'they' are, and even with my own suffering, my heart goes to the other mothers who are grieving the sons they've lost. One mother told me she lost her boy from getting stabbed right in the gut. Completely unjust. So I'm out here at another funeral, like we don't have enough of them to attend, to see another family trying to let go of a life that's been taken unfairly from them.

All these acts of injustice and pure hate crimes and they still don't make the news. No, instead they leave the families to suffer in silence and be bruised. And I'm supposed to continue living this life as the strong black woman? The strong mother, when I'm really seen as the other who's just lost another to being stabbed. How many more of us?

Can I go now?

No response.

I've given my statement..

No response.

Can I go please?

Oh... you'll be in touch?

There's no need

I want to forget this...

Forget this happened...

Forget.

Can I go please?

Statistics

by Shakira Newton

Julia   No, I'm not being overdramatic, 'mate', that's like, what, the sixth, maybe seventh time since I started working here that he's said something dumb like, 'Black people have to try harder to swim 'cause their bones are denser.' And the worst part? He says it with a smirk. With his chest. And no one pulls him up on it. Why should I at my big age, an adult, a lifeguard, still be treated like an 'other', and have to suck it up without saying anything?

But that's just it, ain't it? You say you get it, but I don't think you do.

I didn't realise I was different until others pointed it out. To me people were people. I guess that's the beauty of being brought up mixed. You don't have a preference for, or prejudice against people because of their skin tone or their accent.

I didn't even know what racism was until I was like five and some idiot in the playground started screwing up his face and calling me 'brownie'. Even then I wasn't offended. 'I'm too young to be in the Brownies, I got to Rainbows!' I told him.

Scoffs.

Fucking Girl Scouts.

It obviously got worse when I got into my teens, but it's only now I'm grown that I am really starting to understand just how deep rooted that evil goes. It's not just institutions or 'The Man' trying to keep us down. We ourselves as black people have been training ourselves and each other how to 'act right' and be 'perceived well' for our own safety, forever.

Dad used to take us swimming every Sunday, right. And he'd make us do laps.

Every other kid there was going down the slides or playing with the floats, and me and my sister were out of breath in the deep end, nose and lungs filled with chlorine, as we push ourselves to reach the other side of the 25-metre stretch.

We moaned, obviously, and complained about how unfair it was that other kids got to play whilst we exhausted ourselves. But we still did it. Probably 'cause we knew we'd get chicken nuggets and chips after.

At the time I was more confused about why we had to do laps than why we were the only black people in the place. I was used to us being the only ones around, I guess. Dad said that was exactly it. *That's* why. He didn't want us to be just another statistic. 'The only black kids in town can't swim.'

That's funny, ain't it? He pushed us that hard to prevent us being just another stereotype, and then abandoned us. Now it's not, 'The only black kids in town can't swim.' But, 'A hundred per cent of the black kids in town ain't got a dad.'

How's that for a statistic?

Strong Black Woman
by Gail Egbeson

LULU is a dark skinned young woman in pyjamas and dodo plates. She's scratching her hair as if to get rid of dandruff. This begins to feel soothing.

Lulu I'm not bathing no more. What? Don't even look at me like that. When last did you brush your teeth? If I stink, I stink and if my vagina reeks of the piss I haven't cleaned off for two days straight, then so be it. Come on, I'm black. No matter how many times I bath or hit the shower, this colour ain't going no-where. So let me reek. Let me stink. Let's create what you think. If I wrap my hair, look nice and tight, I still won't get your attention... so let's just let it out, shall we? Be free to be just who you are without unnecessary efforts.

She raises her armpits and uses her fingers to caress the sweat. She takes a sniff.

You smell that? The truth is this. I stink, don't I? My Cancerian soul is freaking out – but... this right here is tactics.

Beat.

Do you just have a problem with black girls or are you a full-on self-racist? One of the basics that hate their own kind. The skin – this melanin cover we hold within. Is my deep shade too ghetto for your 'caramel preference'? Yet traces of you are seen in me and you won't even look at me!

I want your chocolate, those dairy milk arms but 'hey sis' is all you give me. Too dark for your eyes? It's not a surprise you want tin milk with your coffee. Tag us as the bitter, yet ebony strength beats pale beauty. This thing shines – when I cream, so take it, grab on my ashy bum cheeks.

She notices the audience.

Who gave you the right to stare at me? Did I say I wanted to be looked at? I've looked at you and you still glare. It's not your eyes I want.

See, I'm the victim of a duo disease. One you think is all my fault, the other's that fate you can't predict. Fat and dark, the stock that won't sell, not sure which puts him off, but... I just want to be his top vendor, while all inside me craves him.

So he can hit me with the troubles. Bleed me out to flourish... see me as the therapy. I'll take the role to have that hold. I'll break him from within. I'll try and try – till he says goodbye. My strength will carry me through. I'll put this 'Strong Black Woman' to use.

Stubborn
by Max Percy

Juliana Bautista   Enough, sir! If you say those kinds of things again, I'm going to eject you from this ward. You see the signs? Abuse of staff is not tolerated. I'm not Chinese, and even if I was, the Chinese are not to blame for you being sick. If you want to fight, fight the virus. That is the only enemy. I am a qualified nurse. I went to the top med school in Manila. Our nurses are second to none. And we have all left family and friends on the other side the world to work here with you. Also African nurses, Indian, Pakistani, Jamaican, Irish nurses. So no, I am not going to find you another member of staff because today there is only us and we are ready and willed to save your life even if you are not!

So, I will ask you again, what is your name and date of birth? We can't admit you my care until you share your personal details. I have 5 other patients waiting that need my attention. I'm sorry that you were kept waiting. We are very understaffed today. We are under a lot of pressure. All of us. Just like you. Please, your name. Thank you.

I know you are scared. I could hear your breathing in the waiting room. Clots have begun to form in your lungs. How long have you been wheezing? Two days, yes? Was that your daughter who signed you in? She is very beautiful. And even more scared than you. Before you were admitted, she asked me to do my best to look after her dad. I promised her I would make sure that you would be okay. So, you see we cannot let her down. For her we have to work together. As a team. Yes? Okay. Silence is okay. But not more swearing, yes? No more shouting. Save your strength and we will win. Fighters. I like fighters. Your daughter warned me that you can be very stubborn. I said 'Stubborn? He hasn't met me. I'm a Filipina.'

Take A Stand
by Mauricia Lewis

DALEY is tipsy.

Daley 'All black people eat chicken.' That's what you said, is it not? Those are the words that came out of your mouth.

Kisses teeth.

Look at me... Babe! Yoohoo! I'm over here...

Waves hand to gesture where her eyes are.

I know we're all having fun and that, and Dad's giving everyone Guinness punch to celebrate his 'beloved daughter's graduation, but you really can't say shit like that. Jesus Christ, Jez! I don't care, let them all hear me. It's my party. Wooah! Happy graduation to Daley!

Laughs manically.

You know? It took me like... forever to convince my parents to even let you step foot in this house in the first place – 'Don't let that Tory boi step foot inna dis ouse,' that's what he said, you know? And I'm all like, 'Daddy, he isn't just a Tory, he's my boyfriend whom I love, but whose parents also call black people "coloured folk" out of the goodness of their own heart.' And now here you are, cracking misplaced jokes for everyone to hear... I mean, put me in a box and throw away the key, why don't you? Put me in a fucking box, Jez. I wanna be in a box so fucking bad... ughhh... this is so humiliating.

Wallops head in distress.

All you had to do was be my date for the evening and meet some of my family. Maybe even tell a few tales on what it was like growing up in an English public school to rich parents? ...I don't know. Take your pick. Instead, you choose to *embarrass* me in front of my family members by trying to be the next Jack Whitehall and almost shitting yourself in the process.

I'm just disappointed to be honest. We've been together for five months, and all this time I assumed you knew how to behave in front of black people who aren't me. But it seems like I've been mistaken. No! Don't 'fruitcake' me. When someone shows me their true colours, I choose to believe them the first time. I believe you, Jez.

The door's on the latch. If you go now, I'll be able to clean up the mess you've made.

Go!

The Good Son
by Jon Gutierrez

Luis   Dad, for once in your life just listen to me! I refuse
to be another voiceless Latino like the rest of those
damn robots. I want a voice. And I will speak up for
those who need to break away from the chains that
have held us back. Dad! Look at me! I – I am a writer!

All my life I have submitted to your every word
religiously, like God's literal truth. I used to live in
terror of you. Trembling every time I heard your
footsteps in this house, hiding who I really was.
Poor Mum – yes, Dad, you will listen to this! I don't
know how she stomached you, let alone slaved for
you. A foolish, dream-obscuring, miserable old man,
waking up at four, five a.m. every day without fail,
mopping floors and cleaning dirty desks to give us a
chance at the life you never had. I used to look up
to you, but today I realised that you are nothing.
And that you secretly, oh so secretly you don't even
realise, want *me* to be nothing. And that's what I've
been.

Today at 13.00 hours – I don't even know why I
speak like this – At 1.15 today, Boss Dave appears
from nowhere and sits next to me at my desk, inter-
rupting my microwave carbonara because I never
have time to cook anymore, and tells me I'm a
'model staff member', and that the company

exceeded their sales target thanks to my 'resilience and team-player work ethic'. And I thought, 'This is it, Dad, the moment I make you proud. Provider. Winner. Leader of men.'

Then Boss Dave literally pats me on the back and tells me they decided to give the promotion to Charlie Murphy. Looks me in the eye and smiles in my face. Charlie Murphy?! He's been at the company five months! And I actually smile back. Deaf and dumb. Smiling. Sat there at my desk, with everyone celebrating all around me, until it hits me... people like us live and work in a world designed for others to do nothing and win.

So I quit my job. Yes! I quit! My! Job! And it's the best decision I ever made, because I'm tired of trying to live up to the lie. To you and your low expectations. Why did I ever believe any of that bullshit? Yes, I said bullshit, Dad. Fuck the bullshit!

Fuck the bullshit corporations and fuck your 'leader of men' bullshit. I'm a writer, a brilliant writer, maybe a genius, Dad, and thanks to everything I lived through with you, truth, pain and passion will bleed onto every page I write. I'm going to leave a real mark in this world thanks to you and all your rages and mistakes, and if all I get for it is a pat on the back, at least that pat on the back will be mine.

But I'll be damned if let myself or my child, if I ever have one, end up like you.

The Illuminating Discovery
by Saida Ahmed

JADE enters in a wheelchair.

Jade   Hi, my name is...

My name is Jade. *(Nervous smile.)* Yes, I'm sure.

...

It's okay, I'm somewhat lucky in that way. Could you please help me move this chair a bit?

Reluctantly and very politely.

Why would you bolt down an office chair to the floor?

Sees she's being ignored, brushes it off to maintain professionalism.

Well, I'm 22. I've always wanted to be within the performing arts industry, but never as a performer if you know what I mean. I remember when one of your productions toured to my school. I loved it all so much. I enjoyed watching it. That's when I actually knew that I have always wanted to work here at the Illuminate Theatre Company – ever since I was sixteen.

Wow, okay, 'normal' interviewees?

Pause.

Well, I'd say what sets me apart from others is that I'm extremely hard working, in the sense that I work well under pressure. I'm really good at communicating, I'm computer literate, I'm an exceptional listener, not forgetting the fact that as a disabled black woman I'm able to relate to people in different ways and interrelate with people from all walks of life.

I've done a few marketing jobs for my friend's company a while back. I helped my friend's online presence. For example, I helped my friend's company gain over a thousand followers on Instagram and Twitter. Therefore, I'd say I'm more than qualified for this position.

Like I said beforehand, having to be involved in marketing was always the dream. Even from an early age, especially for this company in particular *(ever so kindly)* ...given the fact that it's so inclusive.

Suddenly highly offended.

> Excuse me?
>
> As you can see I don't need a carer.
>
> *(Mutters to herself.)* Is he serious?
>
> ...Yes, I can count. With all due respect, how is this relevant?
>
> It's Jade. It's Jade, you've got it wrong again so I'm

correcting you, it's Jade. J.A.D.E.

Yes, I can spell too – mind blowing, isn't it?

Awkward silence.

Anyway, my chair's pretty fast, but may I ask you yet again how is this question relevant to the job title that I'm applying for?

I beg your pardon? I... I... are you seriously asking me how I use the toilet, are you for real? And you don't even have any accessible toilets anyway, so...

You know what...

Rubs her head continuously out of frustration.

Fuck this! If I did have to wear an adult nappy I'd shit in it and purposely shove it in your rude stupid face!

No, as a matter of fact I don't, because I already have a job. I'm not here for me, and I'm not here for the disgusting questions you've just asked me. I'm here because of someone that you fired on their first day... someone who looks like me. Yes, that's right, I'm a journalist. I've been recording you. I was investigating a disability discrimination case that has been brought to my attention through a reliable source who told me that they applied for a position with your theatre company and had gotten fired on their first day for no good reason. They didn't do anything wrong and were made to feel uncomfortable and unqualified based on discrimination.

Oh, don't you worry, mate, I'm going. Back to work... got an article to finish. Make sure you look out for it. I think you'll find it quite illuminating.

Drives off with a smirk.

The Long Journey Home
by Elander Moore

Shaquille   I knew it was a bad idea. But Mum said I could keep the change if I went, so of course I was out the door quicker than you could say Takeaway Tuesday. The fucking chip shop was closed though, obviously. I remembered that buff Bengali place down the road was open late so I started heading there.

It was pretty quiet on the high street, not much going on except for this one homeless guy shitting into a recycling bin, which I wasn't trying to hang around for. I took a left at the corner shop and I was waiting at the lights I think and... yeah.

I think that's when it happened.

Was proper quick. It came out of a passing car like a dead cigarette butt. Smacked me right between the eyes. Half sung, half shouted like some old football chant.

'NIGGER GO HOME'

The words hung in the air for a bit. Stale and heavy. My brain raced to find some quick reply or blazing insult I could hurl back, but it didn't quite reach my mouth in time. Then as quickly as it came the car had gone. The red man was green and I was off again. Not really that hungry anymore. I headed down past the station and

194

then a quick cut through the park, continued up by the launderette as it began to really get dark.

Head hot in the heat,

fast paced down the street,

kicks pounding the pavement,

my eyes fixed at my feet.

This place is all that I've known.

All I've ever actually seen.

So for me to go back home.

Well, home's where I've always been.

I know every pothole

every puddle and tree.

So tell me where else exactly

Do you intend for me to be

Because yeah

now and then

It feels like I'm stuck in between

Like I've got one foot on land

and another somewhere out at sea

And yeah

I moan and complain

About the grey and the rain

But see these are my ends

and its rivers run within me.

So you just watch me walk on

Through borough and through zone

One pavement crack at a time

On the long journey home.

The Man with the Jacket
by Vy-Liam Ng

Thuong   What's he asking now?

How I got here? And where my parents are?

He wants to check if I'm lying, right? To see if my story is the same as my uncle's?

Well, Miss... (*Looks at translator's badge.*) Miss Anh? Please tell him that we already told the staff when we first got here that I don't know where my parents are.

Tell him that... I think they're dead. Probably. And before he gets angry at me, like the others, tell him I say I 'think' my parents are dead because I don't know, because I didn't see them die, and because I want them to be alive, and all I know is that I've been in this place for weeks now and every time someone new comes through those doors, it's not my mother and it's not my father. Just more random, broken faces with their own stories to tell.

This officer probably thinks those people are lying too. That we're all secret communists or we are here to steal all of the Queen's gold or some bullshit... How is this fair, Miss Anh, to treat us like this? Like criminals?

Breathes.

We were all supposed to meet on the boat... me,
my mother, father and my uncle's family. We were
just supposed to stock the boat over a few days in
secret, and then sail when everyone was ready.
But... but... Then all of a sudden one night it all just
happened – the communists coming for the Chinese.

We heard the shouting, and the shooting getting
closer – to our home. My parents told me to go with
my uncle to the boat and they would meet us there.
I didn't understand why they wanted me to go first
but I trusted them. We waited for hours and hours
in the dark not saying a word. My uncle... with a
hand over his baby's mouth just in case she cried.
his wife was scared that he was going to suffocate
their child, but I could hear her sleeping, her breath
over the yelling in the distance. The gunfire. And
the sound of people dying. I could smell death
coming from the direction of my village. Getting
closer and closer.

So, tell him I said yes, I think my parents are probably dead. And if you think you can translate this
pain that stabs in my chest every time someone
asks me about my family then go ahead and do
that, but do it right! Tell him that with every breath,
I feel like my body wants to cave in on itself and

gather in pieces around my heart and shield it, to protect it from this pain. Tell him I was forced to leave my parents back home to die. And see if you can make this man actually care. Maybe you might even care yourself.

Tell him there is no plan. All they wanted was for me to go to university, finish my studies, learn English. Who knows, maybe it might have been me one day, sitting in your chair, working for some angry British man who thinks the Vietnamese want to steal food out of Hong Kong mouths or something stupid like that. No plan, except that my parents wanted me to live. And though I am here, alive, every moment aches with anger and shame and loneliness. Can you translate that?

The Spark
by Humaira Khan

NOORA, a Pakistani housewife, 20s–mid 30s. In shock.

Noora Even as I stand here packing every item I own I
weep at the fate God has written for me. Your
rages. Your relentless punches.

We both thought I'd stopped resisting long ago, no
fight left in me.

There was never any love in this place where we
lived. No home, just an empty soulless house. Fear
soaked into the walls, and the floors covered in egg-
shells. The puppet and puppet master. Me, foolish
and naïve enough to convince myself that these
purples and blues were tokens of your confused
passion, gifts left all around my broken body. But
the truth is I've been subconsciously anticipating
this very moment, just waiting for enough to be
enough. And today, here it is – the spark. We both
see it and we both know. This is the end.

I am not a lamb! I was not born to be sacrificed, to
push aside my life, choices and freedoms for faith,
culture and all the women before me who couldn't
break their chains. I am more than just your roti-
machine, your sex toy and your punchbag. I am di-
vine and I am human. For so long I have only existed
to please you, to follow you and your demands –

She glances down towards the body.

This was the only way to detach the cord.

I wish my family had allowed me to date. Then I would have learnt about men like you. I wish I could have fucked on the down low, in paid rooms, parks and cars like my friends had. Instead, I was forced to marry your abuse.

I see your eyelids flicker – do you need something? Speak up. Or is just a bit too late? Now that the same baseball bat you used to taunt me with has left its imprint deep in your fucking skull?

The peace is deafening. Finally you're silent. Finally you're stopped. And for the first I'm free to say how glad I am that I couldn't birth you a child. But why say anything? When I can just stand here and take pleasure in watching you take your last few squirming, gurgling breaths. Can you believe it? I'm not even flinching. Sensational. Now you're the one writhing in pain.

And I feel nothing.

Too Black
by Romayn Rose

Lena   You know what? The next train comes in three
        minutes. That's the number of minutes you have to
        convince me that this is still worth it. Or maybe you
        can just cut to the chase and join her at the end of
        the platform. Don't try to add gaslighting to the list
        of shit you have recently been trying to pull cos you
        know that shit don't work on me, Hakeem. You
        always said that was the thing you liked most about
        me, the fact I don't take shit from no one. Look how
        far you're standing from me.

        Isaac? Thought you'd gone home. Do you always
        need to find a girl at the end of the night to help
        you find your way home, huh?

        Isaac makes me laugh. Look at them... both acting
        like they've known each other for time. Can you
        remember the last time we laughed like that? We
        could never get through a day without creasing up,
        but tonight you haven't kissed me... no hug... not
        even your finger grazing the side of my hand out of
        sight in that crowded club. Hakeem! You've been
        more focused on her over there than at me this
        whole night. I thought this was all behind us, I
        thought you had grown up. Isaac! Why you being so
        extra? Everyone on the platform can hear that tune
        from your bruk up phone!

That girl he's with – her dress, it reminds me of that picture of your mum when she was younger. Remember? Remember how everyone said your mum and I looked sooo similar? That was crazy! You know, till this day I've never told your mum why we broke up that time. But then again, how do you tell someone that their son discriminates against them, his girlfriend and ultimately himself. That her son tweeted 'Dark chocolate is always too bitter' and then three vomiting faces. Is that why you're looking at her? Is my complexion a bit too bitter for you to handle tonight?

I'm sorry, baby… please, baby… just look at me!

The train comes in one minute. What's it gonna be?

Too Many Flowers
by Tahys Rodríguez

Sol   I didn't actually want to die, Mama. I just wanted to escape the pain. Go somewhere where my brain could just stop. It's like you're on that last really shitty train home that stops every five minutes, and you can hear the metal against the metal and the screeching, and everyone's talking but you can't make out any words, just white noise, and the toilet door slamming shut as we shake from side to side. I wanted to finally outrun it, find myself somewhere where overthinking doesn't consume me, anxiety doesn't gnaw away at me until I want to peel my skin off, where I don't wake up feeling sick with self-hatred, hatred for this cunt who was pretending to be the perfect dinner guest, partner, employee... Child.

I know, we don't talk about depression or anxiety: those are not Latina people problems. 'Mi amour, you're just a little stressed, it will pass.' We just work harder, as hard as my parents, who gave up everything to move to this country, so that they could have a better life and I could get a seat at the table. Fake-smiling at the right times, pretending to give a shit about the right kind of art. Smart, engaging. Debating politics with just enough edge to be considered a unique thinker. I watched French cinema, hating every second of the gnawing numbness every time I heard myself talk bullshit about Jean Luc Godard and couldn't recognise my own voice. The bile of guilt and shame rising in my throat as I realised that one day I was going to have to kill myself.

It's funny, Mama. Dead people receive so many flowers. Maybe now I'm dead I can be truly loved. I'm not talking pity, or regret, but real love. The kind of love that only comes when you don't need it. The love that comes with death.

Truth Bombs
by Asa Haynes

Donna I'm sorry, what?

Did you just say something about me? I hope the
fuck you did, because I am definitely in the mood to
retaliate today, Derick.

What is at the root of this helpless fascination you
have with me? Is it because my legs are long? Is it
because my lips are full and insisting? Is it because
you long to do a little bit of rumpy-pumpy with me?
Well, unfortunately for you I don't go for white
men, because your penises remind me of uncooked
pork, and I'm Muslim, so it's definitely a no from
me. So consequently all this bullshit chuckling,
sniggering, and mumbling in your dulcet tones into
your off-brand ice coffee as I pass your bombsite of
a desk every morning, has to stop. Yes, that's right,
Derick, I see and hear you, because Black Women
do have ears and eyes.

Oh, Derick darling, why do you look so shocked?
Were you seriously expecting no response to you
poorly stage-whispering, 'That's not her real hair,
she bought that hair from Amazon'?

Did you just expect me to simply sashay past you
day after day for the rest of my hopefully fleeting
period of employment here, just blissfully carrying

on with my pretty little black life? Content to be used as inspiration for a pathetic little whispering worm before you crawl into the meeting room to get savagely castrated in every single team meeting you're allowed to attend?

Oh sorry, have I crossed the line by telling you the truth? We've all seen you retract your big dick energy into that non-existent neck of yours every time you get shut down, which is daily. And every home time, we all watch you go home with your balls in your PE bag, so Mummy can sew them back on while you cry into your raspberry Petit Filous.

Oh don't gape, sweetie, it's not a cute look for you. And while we're on the subject of crossing lines, and since you seem so compelled to generously make endless comments on how nappy and tatty and matted my hair looks, please allow me to re-turn the favour and gift you with some styling tips for your sadly receding hairline. Shave your head. You're not fooling anyone by gelling down your whips.

Amazing. Now we've got that out of the way, let me leave you with this little truth bomb:

I don't really give two shits about what you have to say about me behind closed doors, or while you're at home cooking tuna pasta bake for yourself and your IBS. But while we're pretending to be col-leagues within this establishment, I challenge you to speak your so-called truth with your chest and say it to my face in front of everyone.

But I will tell you this for free: whatever happens next will not be a pretty sight, because that metaphorical castration might suddenly become reality for you. So I'd suggest sleeping with your doors bolted, your windows closed, and both of your piggy little eyes open. Because there are plenty of black women in this establishment who will happily snip off your little pork sausage in the night, fry it up, and serve it to you between two slices of sourdough bread from the local bakery. So think twice before you speak, Derick, or you'll be using a bendy straw to take a piss at the urinals. Got it?

Cool. See you at the next meeting then? It's good to chat.

Twerk For Me
by Talitha Wing

SARAH is stood outside a toilet cubicle, calling through the door.

Sarah 'Kay? Kay? Kayleigh?'

Sarah turns around.

I'm not usually this rude.

'KAAAAAYLEIGH?'

She won't come out of the cubical.

'Come on Kayleigh, open the door.'

Sarah turns around.

'Yeah I know there's a queue, but my friend's in there.'

I know straight away that it's the guy she was dancing with. He had this glint in his eye when he was looking at her. Like he wanted to eat her or something. All wide-eyed and weirdly fascinated.

'What happened?'

Running his fingers through her hair in amazement, like the fucker's never seen braids before.

'Come on.'

She mutters something about feeling embarrassed but I can't quite hear her through the door and the girl getting rowdy behind me.

Sarah turns around.

'Just give me a second, yeah?'

Kay finally opens the door and I squeeze myself into the cubicle before she shuts it again. She's been crying. She says she hasn't – but the mascara all down her face gives her away. I bunch up some toilet roll and wipe her eyes for her. She's so beautiful.

Sarah shouts out.

'We'll be out in one minute!'

Beat.

'He told me to TWERK for him.'

'What?'

'He grabbed me here and said TWERK for me, call yourself black? You're a black girl aren't you?'

I don't really know what happens next. It's like someone's shot an electric current up my spine. I'm standing in this stinking cubicle with my bestest friend in the entire world, who has a hand-print shaped mark on her waist from some guy who thinks that black girls aren't good for anything but twerking. And I want to cry too, but more than that I just, I just want to hurt him. And it's not just him. It's the guy who followed us round the shop earlier. The bar tender who asked where we're really from.

The girls who pushed in front of us in the queue. It's EVERYONE. IT'S FUCKING EVERYONE.

I'm out of the cubicle now, making a bee-line for him. He's tucked in the corner, on to the next girl. I can see him laughing, hands on her waist, whispering something in her ear. And before I know it, I've got my hands on his shoulders. I'm pulling him off of her. I'm shouting some jumbled mess about 'HOW DARE YOU. HOW FUCKING DARE YOU' and he's so confused. I think that's the worst part, he doesn't even know what he's done.

'What? What? You're crazy. You're crazy!' He's a deer in headlights, about to become roadkill.

'YOU TWERK FOR ME, YOU FUCKER! YOU TWERK FOR ME!'

The bouncer grabs me and takes me outside to calm down. I don't need to 'calm down'.

Kayleigh's next to me now, arm round my shoulder, talking to the bouncer, I can't make the words out but eventually he heads back inside.

'Are you okay?' Kay asks. She gives me a hug. 'Let's go home, yeah?'

'Yeah.'

As we're getting our coats I feel a hand on my back. I turn around. It's the girl from the queue. 'Are you alright?' she asks. 'That guy's a massive dick.'

'Yeah, he is.'

And we stand there for a moment. The three of us. In solidarity. This unspoken bond. I like that feeling. It's family.

Typhoon
by Heidi Carmichael

Cez Please, please, please, do not ask me to open this door! I. Am. Exhausted.

But all anyone tells me, is how really tired I'll be when the baby comes! How nothing will ever be the same again and everything will change. I know! It's already changing. It's already changed. I tried to tell you Mum, I tried to tell you Dad. And you were too busy picking out middle names to hear me. While Dad was coming up with the perfect Pinoy nickname, I was screaming behind every smile. 'I'm not ready!!'

I mean, what year is this, for Christ's sake? Who gets married and pregnant at 21? I swear to God if anyone says, 'I told you so', I will sit on them.

Why didn't you stop me? You always stopped me doing everything I ever wanted to. You always said it's such a cliché – the eldest daughter of an Asian family never getting to do what she wants. You always hated being the eldest sibling growing up for that exact reason. Why couldn't you see you did it to me too?

Okay. I love my husband but I've decided we should separate at least until the baby comes. And I don't give a shit if Auntie Glenda or Auntie Gladis or the

other titas gossip about me. We're not even relat-
ed! I need time. Think of it like I'm on holiday. Not
necessarily a holiday from you – I don't hate you all,
not really. I love you. But I just need to be alone
and not see or hear from you – or anyone – and
just... be.

The day we dropped Raya at uni. You were so happy
for her... in a way you've never been that happy for
me. I know, she's the kid, the baby of the family... I
get it. But I swear you have never, never looked at
me like that, even for second. I really thought you'd
get it, Mum, that I was marrying the wrong guy for
the wrong reasons. That you'd step in and tell him
to get lost, send me away to uni to find myself too.
And you didn't.

And ever since that day I'm just... at sea... drifting...
and every time I think I can see land – a fucking
typhoon of... grief just smashes into me. I wish I
could do that thing you all do... acting like nothing
bothers you? Like swans. I'm always below the
surface, splashing around. Drowning.

Beat.

I know – just now – I said I didn't want to hear from
you, but could you let me know if you heard all of
that?

Unrequited
by Sumāh Ebelé

ANGEL: 21 years old.

Three young women who are childhood best friends are sat in a bedroom at a sleepover. They have spent the evening cracking jokes and pouring their hearts out to one another. We're at the point in the night where Angel reveals her insecurities around love to her friends for the first time.

Angel   No stop it!

Just –

Just stop it.

Because it's true.

I mean, let's face it

No but, let's **really** face it here girls.

No one loves the girls like me.   A horny raging bitch of a feminist. Who knows herself so well but not well enough. So self-assured but so insecure and is blatantly, most **obviously** using this façade to cover up the fact that she is feeding off of the pathetic energy and attention that men give her. Just to assure herself that she really might be fine. But, it's just clear she isn't. Right? She's never experienced any form of genuine kindness in her life but **hey ho' here she is. Please** will you **kindly** come and walk over her decapitated body that she can barely stand in. Please, part my legs like the red sea because I can no longer save myself from drowning. Too confident, yet not brash enough. Insecure but my weakness isn't sexy, trust me I know. I know, I'm nothing.   And maybe it's okay,   to be nothing.   I can live with that.   Nothing.   I like nothing.   No boundaries.   No standards.   Nothing to love or live up to.   Just. Nothing.   Much easier than being woman. Right? I think I rather be nothing than woman. Much easier, much much easier

Like I am decapitated. DE-FUCKING-CAPITATED. I'm barely standing. Why is it you can give someone every inch of you and they'll give you nothing back? I feel like my body has been completely ransacked and stolen from. As if I'm a South London JD Sports in the riots or some shit.   I'm tired of believing in a love in which we all know doesn't exist. I'm tired of the fabrication and the constant expectation to be the most amazing version of yourself for someone else. Because people only want you at your best right? So what happens to the women like me, who have never been their best? Who don't actually know what their fucking best is? Do we ever get to know what love is? Will we ever find love? Experience love? Because the only version of myself I've ever known is the fucked up one I have right here, right now and maybe, just fucking maybe. This is it. This might be it. This is me at my best. So what happens to me, I just guess I'll never fall in love? Right?

And I – I don't even mind to be honest. It doesn't even bother me, like I'm fine, I'm **genuinely** fine. If I'm honest, I think we all have such a high expectation and fabricated view of love that none of us know what it actually is. So, I guess, we're all lying I suppose. I guess we're all a bit fucked.

Love.

Shit's stupid.

What I Am
by Julia Hien

Bobbi   What? *I'm* confused?

This is so frustrating! Why doesn't anyone this family *ever* listen to me? I have explained what non-binary means over and over again. What is so difficult about understanding what and who I actually am?

I am Chinese AND Vietnamese right? I am British AND Asian, yes? I can be more than just ONE thing – just like you are someone's parent AND someone's child. And you try to honour both? So this is the same thing. Masculine and Feminine. Both and neither. You see?

'Make sense'? *(Snorts.)* You know what doesn't make sense? This family!

The truth is – sometimes I am envious of my friends who just have a *normal* set of parents. Would you believe that some even proudly display their children's achievements? It's everywhere as soon as you step into their house! Why is it such a taboo for us to just say please or thanks every once in a while?

Or I love you.

Yes. I said it.

I love that every night you always delicately cut up

fresh fruit for us to eat, MaMa. And BaBa, I love that you told everyone in our family that I got into university and I could never stop hearing how proud you were of me from them!

I've always wanted to make you both proud.

Smiles slightly.

And I've also always been a bit confused.

I'd got so used to – well, this. The way we sit in silence when we eat together. The way we automatically take off our outdoor shoes and put on our slippers and move as silent as ghosts as we walk from room to room. The way that when I'm at home, I spend 90% of the time in my room until either of you call me for dinner or want something done.

Smile fades.

And then I learned that there are other ways. To be a family. To be human.

I know that's not how you were raised, but why can't we try something new? Communication. You gave me a western education. You wanted to me learn to ask questions. Well, here's a question: Why can't the feeling of love ever come directly from me to you and you to me?

Hand on heart.

Why can't you say you're proud of me...

Tapping chest gently.

> *...to me?*

> It's so ironic that you don't accept me for who I am and who I want to be, even though you BOTH gave me this. Yes, you did. And it's a gift, whether you're ready to accept it or not. I am what I am and I LOVE WHO I AM!

Wiping eyes.

> Even if my parents don't.

Swallows, exhales.

> I have always been grateful that you both gave me this life – And my name, Bobbi!

Laughing and crying.

> You knew. Be honest – you knew – and I always will be grateful. But neither of you get to decide who I am. And when you're ready to accept who I am. The child you made. I'll be right here.

> Being me.

Where Are You Really From?
by Antonia Kleopa

*AALIYAH – Late 20s – Mediterranean – London accent
(North/South)*

Aaliyah   I'll stop you right there, before you dig yourself a
hole. Where are you from? I know you grew up in
London but – where are you really really from? Are
you sure you're fully white? Quick way to tell – do
you even tan in summer or do you just turn proper
red? Nah, your small white features give it away.
And wow – your hair is so – can I? *(She attempts to
touch his hair.)* Ah, I've never actually touched
straight hair before, it's so exotic! I bet you get a lot
of looks, proper white boy ain't ya! This restaurant
must be different for you (since it's cultured). How
do you feel eating here? I bet you're gonna choose
a dish without ANY seasoning. You can't handle all
that spicey spicey huh?! I should probably tell you...
I have never been with a white man. I guess it's a
Mediterranean privilege of mine actually, not having to venture out into the wild. *(Quietly.)* I've heard
you white men are real goers – is that true?! Sorry,
that's really stereotypical of me to assume isn't it?
(Beat.) Yeah. Yes it fucking is. Is it too difficult for
you to ask me? Instead of just assume based on
your guessing game. The colour of my skin. The texture of my hair. My dark features. Yes, in fact – I do
get looks. Do you think us 'exotic' women would

fuck you differently? It's my time to guess now. Or is it that you'd enjoy me by your side, just to show that you're mixing with a bit of culture. Oh come on, white boy, speak up! Which box do you tick when you have to fill out a form? You've got about four different types of white to choose from – how very fortunate. Then you've got us Mediterraneans, who don't exist, apparently! I do have one option though – the 'Other' box. Do you see me as an 'Other'? It isn't hard to partition those pale lips of yours to say something, since you've ignorantly said enough – so answer me. Better to just label us as something, right? Since it's too problematic for people like you to acknowledge who we actually are? Oh, look you're going proper red – I was right – you do turn into a fucking tomato! Best to date a woman who looks exactly like you from head to toe, hmm? Then she can join your little white-roast-dinner-family without having to answer twenty-one questions from Mummy and Daddy about where she comes from, because guess what – she won't have to. I wouldn't adjust who I am for nobody – so go ahead, look at me and wonder. Fantasise – when you take a good hard look at me. Oh – go on, shake your head at me! That's it, mmm! Why don't you give your little wiener a shake too? I'll do an 'exotic' dance for you – come on! Oh – aww – bye then! Go on, walk away – and whilst you're there let me see you shake that teeny tiny little white arse of yours!

Where's Home for You
by Sarel-Rose Madziya

Tinashe   That question is so stupid.

Simplistic.

Basic.

On the one hand I'm from here, I grew up here. My first kiss was here. First time I got stopped and searched, here.

I only remember it because apparently I 'matched the description of a suspect who had fled the scene'. Later found out that the 'suspect' was a 27 year old black man... I was 14. But I guess they got the black part right. That's the only part they ever get right.

On the other hand, look at me! No, actually look at me, I must be bat shit crazy or delusional to even think I'm from an Anglo blood line.

No sweetie, I'm black, Sorry. We were cargoed here like exotic fruits.

Where am I from? Where are you from?

One could argue we're all from Africa, scientifically. Except when my auntie sees me at gate 3 I hear her whisper to my mum something along the lines of... your children are so white. Even on the motherland, where I'm from, they don't see me as enough. Like being born there wasn't enough. Like knowing the culture isn't enough. Eating the food, singing the songs isn't enough. What? You want blood, you want a living sacrifice around a campfire to prove my loyalty, auntie?

My favourite is when the caucs get fancy with it, like, 'and where's home for you?'

Or

'So, what's your background?'

Dear Haleys of this world, do you have to give a detailed ancestry DNA to preface every conversation?

I would love to know about your Viking great great grandfather.

Every interview, networking event, wedding, first date, baby shower, birthday, graduation even fucking bar mitzvah it's the same, boring, mundane, tone deaf shit.

And so it creeps in
the self-doubt
thick
strangles you like a noose.

You feel like an object, like the only value you hold is that of your ancestors, which you had zero impact in. Who cares that I was able to teach myself how to speak Spanish after a gut-wrenching break up, that I volunteered In Mozambique for six months, took part in a drug testing trial while broke at uni, managed to run a 5k with a tapeworm lodged in my stomach and learnt sign language because I fucked a guy who just so happened to be hard of hearing on a night out?

And guess what that motherfucker asked me? *(Signing and speaking.)* 'Do you speak English?' I regret not calling him out on it because the shag was not worth the racial microaggression.

But I was 19 and dumb – said yes – and snogged his face off.

White Receipt
by Yuyu Wang

BLUE: non-white, not from the UK.

Blue   I hate receipts. Any kind of receipts. I hate them all.

It's my first day in London and I rush all the way towards Tate Modern – you know, that gallery at Southbank, world class, avant garde, full of wonderful arts. That's why I'm here, flying all the way across the ocean to be here. I love this country! I love it all!

There are security guards at the door, of course. They protect the arts.
'Sure you can check my bag. Not much in here. Just my camera, passport and some cash. Nothing suspicious I promise you. I am a good immigrant.'

Now I'm inside Tate Modern. Wow. Look at it. Look at the art.

There is this white receipt beautifully exhibited on the wall. I keep staring at it. Wow. This is what you call art. Art is everywhere, a white receipt on the wall.

FYI that receipt is called 'Monochrome Till Receipt (White)' by Ceal Floyer. You can google it. It is a list of purchased goods, about this long, this wide. And it is *so* white. It's a white list of white things that are white, or have 'white' in their names.

I will never find myself on that list you know. I'm not white. I don't have a white name. I can still add the word 'white' to my name but my parents would be so mad.

I'm so jealous of that white receipt. Everything about it is white but I am not.

Most people might just see the price, the capitalism, the jokes on modern art, but I can only see the whiteness, the privilege, the hierarchy of shopping trips. Some people get to shop at Waitrose but some people are stuck in Tesco. I am stuck in Tesco.

I feel this strong urge inside me to tear the white receipt apart, draw a rainbow on the wall, write in capital letters 'I AM NOT WHITE' and add 'NOW I'M ON THE WALL' next to it. People will applaud and I will take a bow. Security guards will rush towards me but I will not run. They will take me down and rub my face against the cold floor. I will scream at the top of my voice, 'Put more colours on the wall! More colours on the wall!' until they gag me and tie me up and drag me away. I will be fined and punished and evicted from this country. I have no power to fight to stay, but my art will stay on the wall.

The white receipt is for £70.32. Art is expensive. About a decade ago Tate spent £30,000 to buy that white receipt. Art *is* expensive.

That expensive pain burning in my chest. I love London art so much. But it won't love me back.

Work Party
by Chantelle Alle

Melanie   Who in this room is darker than me? Anyone? Dave, I know *you're* not about to raise your hand right now. Anyone at all? *(Beat.)* That's right. No one. No one's skin in this room is darker than mine. I am the only black person in the office. Well, me and Dave over there, if you wanna get 'technical'. But your mum's Caucasian, isn't she, Dave? Or is it your dad? I can't even remember which parent you said it was because I was too busy watching you pour a ridiculous amount of sugar in your coffee. Why the hell do you use so much sugar, Dave? You know everybody in the office talks about it, right? I don't know how many more times poor Hannah needs to pop into Tesco's because you've left none for the rest of us.

No, no, no, I haven't had enough, actually. *I* brought this bottle of wine, so I can have as much as I like, thank you very much. You know, you have this way of talking to me. Everyone single one of you. I swear, it's actually amazing when I think about it, because you *all* do it. How can I describe it…? Patronising? Condescending? Bullshit?

I mean, some of you I have to give credit to because you're slyer with your approach, but the rest of you, my God! Emma, why is it that every time I come into work, you must make a show of what I'm wearing? 'Ooh girl, you look fierce today!', 'Yass, slay Queen!' Every day. Every. Single. Fucking. Day. At first I was flattered, but it didn't take long before it became annoying! I actually came in one time and purposely dressed like a homeless person just to see what you'd say. And lo and behold, along came that finger click and wave of imaginary pixie dust in the air as you told me how fabulous I looked. You raggedy, bitch.

And I don't know what you're sniggering about, Mark, because if you ever reach out to touch my hair again, I will kill you dead. I do not care that you are my manager. I don't give a shit. Yes, I might come in with my afro one day, and maybe braids down to my arse the next. But can we try not to throw a party about it? I change my hairstyle as often as Hannah has to go and get more fucking sugar. So, perhaps we should steer this energy towards her, doing the Lord's work so we can all have our teas and coffees! She wasn't even invited today. God forbid we invite the intern to this magnificent party! Who on earth would she talk to?

Funnily enough, it would have been me. Because unless it's about Stormzy or Beyoncé, the conversations I have with you guys never seem to get that far. Well, other than when I'm correcting your pronunciation of my last name. Or that time one of our clients referred to me as 'the coloured woman who hosted the presentation'. 'Coloured?' Seriously? And you never even said a word, Dave. Nothing. I should have known from that time someone said that you could pass off as white and you smiled. Smiled! Like it was a compliment.

Pause.

For future reference, and actual decent conversation: I enjoy swimming on Saturday mornings, evening strolls by the Thames and gardening – for those of you who didn't know, which would be all of you, since you've never asked. Then there's photography! My photography.

In fact, you know what? I'm actually a better photographer than I am a data analyst.

Thinks.

I quit.

Yammin on a Patty
by Alice Straker

Pete   So there I was; yammin' on a patty whilst waiting
for the bus which was, shock horror, late yet again. I
don't know why, but after a patty I always feel like I
can take on the world. Mid yamming, I clock Karissa
from a mile away. Ruby red hair and a tight little
waist – proper naughty! She has these mahoosive
out of proportion hips that don't correlate with the
rest of her body. Like none of these Coca-Cola
bottle Kardashian type hips, these are next level
child-bearing hips. That's what I've always liked
about her though, a real woman! She just always
looks… fire! Whenever I see her something takes
over, memories flood back in and I realise that
adolescent animalistic feeling is still stuck solidly in
my head – like chewing gum underneath a school
table. Must be those ferret moans kicking in.

Anyway, as she's getting closer I notice her pushing
something. At first I thought it was one of those
little granny carts, you know the ones that you can
fill your shopping with? All the rage these days, not
to mention they're actually proper useful! Only
went and dropped the patty when I realised she
was pushing a pickney in a pram! I didn't know what
to say, so we don't say nothing. This girl just has to
look at me a certain way and I'm a proper cheese

melt! We sit on adjacent sides of the bus and I'm trying to come up with something. And she's all calm. And then boom. I'm just full on staring at this baby, like this little innocent human is blissfully unaware of this mad world that we're living in. And Karissa says, all soft like... 'Her name's Jade.' and I just know that Jade is mine. Boy. I don't know what to say. I don't know what to feel. Guilt? Yeah. Guilt. My missus would be crushed, broken if she knew. But what about this kid? I've missed out on the first months of this precious baby girl; my daughter's life. Milestones gone, evaporated like rain off tarmac on a summer's day. Disappointed? I know I'm a cheat but there's just something about being around Karissa and Jade that makes me feel like home. And I don't know what to do. I need another patty.

Also available from Team Angelica Publishing

Prose

'Reasons to Live' by Rikki Beadle-Blair
'What I Learned Today' by Rikki Beadle-Blair
'Faggamuffin' by John R Gordon
'Colour Scheme' by John R Gordon
'Souljah' by John R Gordon
'Drapetomania' by John R Gordon
'Hark' by John R Gordon
'Fairytales for Lost Children' by Diriye Osman
'Cuentos Para Niños Perdidos' – Spanish language edition of 'Fairytales',
    trans. Héctor F. Santiago
'The Butterfly Jungle' by Diriye Osman
'Black & Gay in the UK' ed. John R Gordon & Rikki Beadle-Blair
'Sista! – an anthology' ed. Phyll Opoku-Gyimah, John R Gordon & Rikki
    Beadle-Blair
'More Than – the Person Behind the Label' ed. Gemma Van Praagh
'Tiny Pieces of Skull' by Roz Kaveney
'Fimí sílè Forever' by Nnanna Ikpo
'Lives of Great Men' by Chike Frankie Edozien
'Lord of the Senses' by Vikram Kolmannskog

Playtexts

'Slap' by Alexis Gregory
'Custody' by Tom Wainwright
'#Hashtag Lightie' by Lynette Linton
'Summer in London' by Rikki Beadle-Blair
'I AM [NOT] KANYE WEST' by Natasha Brown
'Fierce' – a monologue anthology ed. Rikki Beadle-Blair
'Common' – a monologue anthology ed. Rikki Beadle-Blair

Poetry

'Charred' by Andreena Leeanne
'Saturn Returns' by Sonny Nwachukwu
'Selected Poems 2009-2021' by Roz Kaveney
'The Great Good Time' by Roz Kaveney
'Perfect.Scar' by Robert Chevara